Praise for
A Year in Paradise: How We Lived Our Dream

" . . . . a delightfully unpretentious odyssey . . . . a charming yarn,
sure to inspire sofa sailors of all ages . . . . This book is chock full
of useful details."
—NEWSDAY

" . . . . informative, easy to read, and entertaining . . . . an enjoyable
book. If you have ever wanted to do this, you must read this book.
The Wattersons tell the good and the bad . . . . they detail places,
sights, sounds and people. Short, sweet, and a real gem."
—INLAND SEAS

"A delightful and informative read on cruising the Intracoastal
Waterway, plus a tiny sub-plot: the partnership of a 60-something
married couple taking the voyage of HIS dreams. Deftly written."
—WORCESTER TELEGRAM & GAZETTE

" . . . . one of the most practical 'how to's' I have ever read. A really
encouraging documentary of someone who has been there, done
that, and lived to tell about it. About three pages into the book, this
powerboater forgot that it was a book by a sailboater. Without a
doubt, it is a book written by a cruiser for other cruisers."
—GREAT LAKES CRUISER

"The combination of the Wattersons' straightforward style and
practical, learn-from-our-mistakes advice leaves the reader with the
message: 'if we could do it, so can you!' *A year in Paradise* is
equal parts entertainment, advice, and inspiration for those who
dream of spending a year on board."
—SOUNDINGS

"This book details the Watterson's trip from start to finish, including all the planning involved. This is a 'we did it, so can you!'
book."
—OHIO MAGAZINE

"A wonderfully entertaining book . . . ."
—LONG ISLAND ENTERTAINMENT

A Year in Paradise:
How We Lived Our Dream

STEPHEN WRIGHT WATTERSON

A Year in Paradise
How We Lived Our Dream

EPC
EAGLE CLIFF PRESS
CLEVELAND OHIO

A Year in Paradise: How We Lived Our Dream

Published by Eagle Cliff Press, 31346 Lake Road, Cleveland, Ohio 44140-1070.

Typesetting and composition by the publisher. The text of this book is composed in Amethyst and Amethyst Light Italic, with display type set in Amethyst, Algonquin Italic, and Arial

Book design by the author. Photographs and maps by the author except where otherwise noted. Front cover photograph by William McIntyre; back cover photograph by Jacquie Brown.

Printed by Activities Press, Inc., Mentor, Ohio

First printing May 2001
Second printing April 2002

Publisher's Cataloging-in-Publication
(Provided by Quality Books, Inc,)

Watterson, Stephen Wright.
A year in paradise : how we lived our dream / Stephen Wright Watterson. -- 1st ed.

p. cm.
LCCN: 00-192882
ISBN: 0-9706167-0-8

1. Boats and boating--Atlantic Intracoastal Waterway. 2. Boats and boating--Atlantic Coast (U.S.) 3. Boats and boating--Great Lakes Region. 4. Atlantic Intracoastal Waterway--Description and travel. 5. Atlantic Coast (U.S.)--Description and travel. 6. Great Lakes Region--Description and travel. 7. Watterson, Stephen Wright--Journeys. 8. Watterson, Margaret--Journeys. I Title.

GV776.A84W38 2001   797.1'24'0974
                    QBI00-939

ACKNOWLEGEMENTS

The people most responsible for this book are those friends and family members who read and enjoyed the newsletters that Margaret and I published during our adventure, and who encouraged me to put them in book form. There are just too many of you to name here, but you know who you are and I thank all of you.

I am grateful to Kerry Watterson who read the manuscript for consistency, and to Margaret Watterson for her many readings and advice. I am also indebted to Dura Curry, who read this work in progress and offered numerous valuable suggestions.

The Owl and the Pussycat went to sea
    In a beautiful pea-green boat:
They took some honey, and plenty of money
    Wrapped up in a five-pound note.

They sailed away, for a year and a day,
    To the land where the bong tree grows . . .

And hand in hand, on the edge of the sand,
    They danced by the light of the moon,
        The moon,
        The moon,
    They danced by the light of the moon.

Edward Lear

Paradise is not a place . . . . .
    it is a state of mind.

Anonymous

CONTENTS

Introduction   *1*

Chapter 1 Lake Erie to the Hudson River   *9*

Chapter 2 Hudson River to Chesapeake Bay   *23*

Chapter 3 Chesapeake Bay   *39*

Chapter 4 North Carolina   *51*

Chapter 5 The Low Country   *67*

Chapter 6 Down the Sunshine Coast   *83*

Chapter 7 Turnaround   *99*

Chapter 8 Homeward Bound   *111*

Chapter 9 Where the Pel'kins and Porpoises Play *123*

Chapter 10 The Story of Uncle Sam   *139*

Chapter 11 The Last Hurrah   *151*

Appendix   *161*

Introduction

Who Called This Meeting, Anyway?

THIS BOOK IS ABOUT a year-long cruise that my wife, Margaret, and I took on our 30-foot sailboat, *Witch of Endor*, from Sandusky, which is near Cleveland, Ohio, to the Florida Keys and back. We were in our middle sixties, and we had owned sailboats for about ten years. The trip was a real adventure for us, and the realization of a dream; the purpose of this book is to convey what it was like to actually live that dream.

To keep family and friends informed and amused during our cruise, we published a series of newsletters, using a laptop computer and printer we had on board the boat. The newsletters were running commentaries on our experiences and impressions as we explored the waterways of the US East Coast. This book is based on those newsletters.

Here's How it all Started

LIKE MOST SAILORS, I had for years dreamed of taking a long cruise, and I was really attracted to the idea of going to Florida via the Intracoastal Waterway. (The Intracoastal Waterway is a route for boats to travel up and down the eastern seaboard in relatively protected waters).

The Florida Keys, with Key West as the southernmost point of the continental United States, seemed to be a reasonable goal and a pleasantly logical turnaround point for such a cruise.

I did not dream of ocean voyaging to distant lands. Ocean cruising requires knowledge, skills, and aptitudes that I lacked and had little prospect of acquiring. While it is true that one hears of people with little or no prior experience sailing across an ocean (and often arriving on the other side), I didn't feel that I had the time or resources to prepare my boat or myself for such an undertaking (read: chicken. Actually, the problem was lack of experience. I would not want to go offshore without doing it first with an experienced blue-water sailor). Another reason for not seriously considering an ocean voyage was that there was no chance of Margaret agreeing to accompany me.

Coastal cruising, on the other hand, while challenging, calls for skills that I possessed. A trip down the Intracoastal Waterway (ICW) would be similar to our normal summer weekend cruising among the Lake Erie Islands, and our occasional two-to-three week cruise on the Great Lakes. The differences would be that in the case of the Waterway trip, we would be living on board for an extended period instead of for just a few weeks, and we would of course be continually confronted with new situations. (In hindsight, the experience was only remotely similar to what we were used to. The challenges far exceeded expectations. But ocean voyaging it was not.)

This adventure had been a dream for a long time, and Margaret and I would sometimes pretend that we were actually going to do it, and talk about it as if it was real. Although deep down inside I was committed to the idea, on the surface I was not sure it was going to really happen. Yet it seemed to become more and more tangible, although still just talk, until one day we asked ourselves whether we were *really* going to do this, and the answer was . . . . *Yes!*

Margaret's one condition, which I readily accepted, was that we take a cat with us. We agreed on a duration (about a year), a destination (to the Florida Keys and back), and a departure date (mid-July, a year and a half hence)—and the rest is history.

This map illustrates the extent of *Witch of Endor's* cruise from the Cleveland area in Ohio to the Florida Keys and back.

Getting Ready

D URING THE YEAR AND A HALF leading up to our departure, I did a number of things to the boat like increasing water storage capacity, and adding batteries and refrigeration, and I also accumulated the charts and cruising guides which we would need. In addition, there was a myriad of other tasks like budgeting and thinking through issues such as bill paying, mail, insurance, and cash flow. These and other details of planning and preparation are covered elsewhere, but I want to briefly mention mail and a couple of other matters now so that references later in the narrative will make more sense.

We live in Bay Village, Ohio, which is a western suburb of Cleveland. Our son and daughter-in-law, Stewart and Ellen, live nearby. During the year of our cruise, they collected our mail, paid bills, discarded junk mail, and sent us packages of real mail every three to five weeks to marinas and Post Offices along the way as we arranged to receive them.

Kerry and Joann, another son and daughter-in-law, live in suburban Washington, DC, up the Potomac River from Chesapeake Bay. With family and friends along the way in Staten Island, NY; New Jersey; Washington, DC; South Carolina; and Georgia, we were well situated with folks to visit as we worked our way south.

Pukka the Sea Kitty

N OW WE COME TO the matter of the cat. I am not sure why Margaret conditioned her participation in this adventure on our acquisition of a cat. Our family has included a number of cats over the years—animals to which I have generally been indifferent—and in recent times I have discouraged Margaret from getting another one. It could be that she simply saw an opportunity to get the pet she wanted, knowing how much I wanted to go on

Witch of Endor sailing on Lake Erie. Photo courtesy of Scott Schaefer.

the trip. It could also be that she believed that a third creature on board, albeit feline, would provide a sympathetic ally when needed, although I could not image such a need arising. And, of course, it is possible that she thought it would be nice to have the fun and companionship that a friendly kitty would provide, although, again, I didn't see the need. After all—*I* was going to be there. (I suspect that in the fullness of time—which here means before too many pages pass under our keel—Margaret will illuminate these matters with her characteristic directness.)

And so, soon after our decision to do the cruise, it came to pass that we presented ourselves to the City of Cleveland Animal Protective League. There, we made our choice based on sex (F), size (small), age (young), alertness (very), and appearance (pretty). The kitty was named Pookie, which, although suitable as a nickname, was, I felt, lacking in dignity and too informal for an aspiring sea-going cat. Accordingly, I re-named her Pukka.

We did several things to prepare Pukka for her new life as a sea kitty. We got her a harness and leash so she could be tethered to the boat—she would not be able to slip out of a harness as easily as a collar. Because you cannot have a dish of water sitting on the floor of a boat, Margaret trained her to drink from the kind of water dispensing gadget that you hang in a rabbit or gerbil cage. (She used water mixed with the water from water-packed canned tuna in decreasing strength over several days. Brilliant!) We had her spayed and declawed (front only). Her litter box tucks neatly into a corner of the head (bathroom) compartment on the boat.

We accustomed Pukka to the *Witch of Endor* by taking her with us on our normal two to three day stays on the boat. When we put her in her carrying case to go to the marina it was clear that she was thinking, "*Oh shoot . . . we're not going out there again!*" (There is, I think, a smidgen of alley cat in this animal). However, we persevered, and she soon was traveling like a trooper. It took her a while to get used to the boat's diesel engine, and she would remove herself as far away from the noisy iron beast as she could— which meant up in the forepeak where she had a snug little refuge. Boats have lots of places for cats to disappear in.

After a while she seemed to accept the idea that she had two homes—one that was big and spacious and satisfyingly stable, with trees and grass and chipmunks outside (she's an indoor cat), and another one that was a lot smaller, pointy at one end, likely to be bouncing around and leaning over (normal angle of heel for most sailboats underway is 10 to 20 degrees), with water and big menacing birds outside.

Margaret Speaks

IN THE PERIOD before our departure, I left it to Steve to do all the mechanical things to the boat, as well as the planning, budgeting, and all that. After all, this was his show, and maybe *he* was going on an adventure—*I* was going on a cruise. Nevertheless, I did think about food provisioning, meals, what utensils and kitchen gear to bring, clothes, and where to stow it all.

Regarding my reasons for wanting a cat on the cruise, Steve is right on all counts. I also thought it might be useful to have a referee on board.

Hmmm. . . .

Lake Erie to the Hudson River

East to the Canal!

THERE ARE TWO WAYS to go by boat from Sandusky, Ohio to the Hudson River, and both involve transiting canals. One of the canals is short and scary and the other is long and fun. The short and scary one is the Welland Canal that goes across a narrow piece of Ontario, Canada and connects Lake Erie with Lake Ontario. It is scary (at least for us), because it is the big ship canal. It is used by the ocean-going freighters (known on the Lakes as "Salties"), which enter the Great Lakes by the St. Lawrence Seaway and travel to Cleveland, Toledo, Detroit, Chicago, Milwaukee, and Duluth, and also by the Great Lakes bulk carriers (known as "Lakers").

It is not that we dislike the big ships; we deal with them all the time in our usual Great Lakes cruising. It is that the large and very turbulent locks in the Welland can present a severe challenge to elderly couples in small boats. The authorities require that recreational boats

Our route took us clear across upstate New York from Buffalo to Troy and then down the Hudson River to New York City.

have three line handlers on board—not in itself a fatal drawback because you can hire one for the passage or borrow someone from another boat with excess crew— but it does give you a clue about what to expect.

The Welland Canal route to the Hudson River takes you east on Lake Ontario to Oswego, New York— most of the length of Lake Ontario. At Oswego, you enter the New York State Barge Canal System (the Erie Canal) about half-way across New York, and then follow the Erie Canal eastward to the Hudson.

The second route, and the route of choice for us, is to enter the Erie Canal directly from Lake Erie at Tonawanda, New York, which is just a little north of Buffalo on the Niagara river. This leads to a fabulous experience, enjoying the lazy summer days while poking along across upstate New York. Yes, there are locks on the Erie Canal, 35 of them between Tonawanda and

Troy, which is 350 miles to the east on the Hudson River. However, they are relatively tame and only a few of them pose much of a challenge.

Party Time in Sandusky

B UT I AM GETTING ahead of myself. I want to tell you a little about the festivities surrounding our departure, because it was so much fun.

Our family and friends were overwhelmingly supportive of our venture. Many, especially among our boating friends, were envious; others were probably just glad to get me out of their hair, even if only for a year. A few of our non-boating friends, I think, were concerned about Margaret's welfare. We were presented with a mariner's St. Christopher medallion, which I mounted on the instrument panel in the navigation station of the boat.

The entire departure experience was one big party. First, a few days before the actual push-off in mid-July, Stewart and Ellen threw a marvelous Bon Voyage party for us in a beautiful party room in a marina venue, which was attended by many friends. Then, on the morning of our departure day (departure having been sagely scheduled by the Skipper for a Saturday noon), dock-mates and friends at our home marina in Sandusky staged a Bon Voyage breakfast at the marina pavilion. Then, later in the morning, after gorging ourselves on all kinds of breakfast goodies, our Miata Club friends arrived (yes, Margaret belongs to a *Miata* Club!*)*, with streamers, leis, and champagne. Wow!

Our floating dock was practically awash under the weight of this mass of partying humanity as, with glasses raised and streamers flying, all gathered around our slip to watch as we cast off the lines and backed into the channel. We motored over to our first stop, the pump-out station, accompanied by our boisterous well wishers and a deafening chorus of boat horns. After pumping out the holding tank under the gratuitous gaze of our gaping gallery, we departed, trailing colorful paper streamers in the water and accompanied by a cacophony of clamoring horns.

As the festivities faded astern, we looked ahead across Sandusky Bay out to the open water beyond, and knew that we really had to go. So we went.

Sailing Lake Erie

OVER THE NEXT few days *Witch of Endor* sailed east on Lake Erie, stopping at Lorain, Cleveland, Fairport Harbor, and Ashtabula in Ohio; Erie, Pennsylvania; and Dunkirk and Buffalo, in New York. We are not overnight sailors; these are daily runs of 25 to 40 miles. Except for high winds between Erie and Dunkirk, we had good weather. Our home yacht club membership enabled us to tie up at clubs in these ports, and all were pleasant and hospitable. We had visited most of them in the past.

There is a story attached to each of these stays, but I am going to do you a favor and only mention one. The Westlake Yacht Club at Lorain, Ohio is located in a marina up the Black River, above the Route 6 bascule bridge. (This is the type of drawbridge that has two leaves that rise up and when down meet in the middle). Our mast would not fit under that bridge—we needed to have the bridge open for us. The procedure for this is to hail the bridge tender on the radio to find out what his opening schedule is, and to ask him (or her) to open. If you know that the bridge opens on demand, you can also give him a horn signal—one long and one short, which is the request to open.

Under power and with our sails furled, we moseyed on up to the bridge. I hailed the bridge tender on the hand-held VHF radio that we keep in the cockpit, but he did not respond. I hailed him on channel 9, channel 13, and channel 16. There was no response. Now, in a boat you cannot just stand still and stay in the same place, as you can in a car. There's usually some wind or current that is going to push you around to someplace you don't want to be; you have to keep moving in order to be able to steer and maintain control of the boat. So I kept circling, hailing the bridge tender on the radio and giving him horn signals, but I still got no response. I could see the guy up there in his little house. I was waving, calling on the radio, and blasting with the horn, and I could see him looking at me, but I didn't even get a wave.

All of this was being observed by a growing gallery on the shore, and Margaret, who can hear better that I can, finally got the message from them that we needed to call the bridge by its full correct name, or he would never open it for us. *Good grief!* I had been calling it the Route 6 Bridge, the Lorain Black River Bridge, and all sorts of other fully appropriate and suitable names. I do not remember what the actual "full correct name" is (my mind has blocked it out)—it is probably something like The Alphonse J. Kowalski Memorial Highway Bridge or whatever.

Margaret got the correct name from our shoreside helpers. I called the bridge tender, and the *instant* the words were out of my mouth the bells rang, the red lights flashed, the gates went down, the traffic stopped, the bridge rose majestically, and we motored serenely through, accompanied by the waves and cheers of our adoring audience. Oh well.

We Become a Motor Vessel

SAILBOATS TRANSITING the Erie Canal need to have their masts taken down and stowed on their decks so they can fit under the many bridges which cross the canal. Typically, the bridges in the towns along the way are only five or six feet above the water. Although the bridge tenders raise these bridges, they are not raised very high. Between Tonawanda and Three Rivers Point (about halfway across the canal), many of them rise to a height of only 15½ feet above the water level. This is

Margaret—on the bench, right—catching up with her knitting while we were tied up next to the bridge at Spencerport along the canal. *Witch of Endor* is on the left, partly out of the picture.

high enough for most recreational powerboats, but not sufficient clearance for sailboat masts, so sailboat masts have to come down.

Large powerboats needing more than 15½ feet of clearance take the Welland route; on the eastern half of the canal the controlling clearance is 20 feet above the water level. (The *really* big guys have to use the St. Lawrence Seaway.)

On our way to Tonawanda, which is the town at the mouth of the canal where you take your mast down, we stayed at the Buffalo Yacht Club. While there (a wonderful club, very friendly, and with great food), we removed the sails, the boom and the bimini. The sails went into the cockpit locker, and the boom and bimini supports were secured on deck. We planned to get up to Tonawanda the next day, have the mast unstepped (taken down) at Wardell's Boatyard there, spending the night at Wardell's, and maybe do a little grocery shopping before setting out on our canal adventure.

All went as planned. Mr. Wardell unstepped the mast with his crane, and we got it stowed fore and aft on the mast supports (I had built them before departure; they were stored in the cockpit locker), with shrouds and stays bundled up with the mast as neatly as possible. Wardell's is not a place that one would choose to spend one's holiday, but it gets the job done. The cost is reasonable considering that the charge of $2.50 per foot of mast length includes a night's dockage with electricity.

With her mast down, *Witch of Endor* became a motor vessel; we would not be raising sails until the mast went up again on the Hudson River, about two weeks later.

We were well prepared for the Erie Canal. I had sent to the New York State Canal Corporation for a package of guides, maps and other useful information, and we had on board *A Cruising Guide to the Northeast's Inland Waterways,* written by the Rumseys and published by International Marine. We also had the NOAA Chartbook covering the eastern part of the canal. In addition, we used the excellent *Waterway Guide, Northern Edition.*

There is a charge for going through the locks; for transiting the entire canal, you buy a season permit at the first lock. The fee for a boat our size was $75.

Oh Those Lazy Summer Days!

I SIMPLY CANNOT TELL YOU how much we enjoyed our trip across this canal, especially the western half. The canal towns, with their downtown terminal walls, and their grassy, park-like places to tie up for the night (often with electricity and water available), compete with one another to see which can be the most hospitable to transiting boaters. The townspeople and the bridge tenders take pride in the appearance of the canalside park areas. Volunteers maintain the grounds around the locks also, which are sometimes downtown but more usually between towns. The locks compete for prizes awarded for the most attractive flowerbeds and landscaping.

Left, *Witch of Endor*, with her mast secured on deck and fenderboard in place, ready for her transit of the canal. Right, the bridge at Fairport.

There is a strong sense of history in these towns, and their names resonate with their canal heritage—Lockport, Middleport, Spencerport, Brockport, Fairport.

The lock and bridge tenders were helpful and friendly. They would often get the name of our boat, and ask how far we were going that day so they could call ahead to let their colleagues know we were coming. One of them told us that the reason they got the boat name and kept track of us was so that if our children called they would know where we were. (Good grief! —here we were trying to get away to have a little adventure, and these guys were going to *sic our kids on us!*)

The areas surrounding the locks also provide pleasant places to tie up for the night, some with picnic facilities and electrical hookups. Local families come out to watch boats locking through, so there is often the chance to chat. We got the feeling that many folks would rather be doing what we were doing than to be watching on the sidelines. Calling out "Is this the way to Key West?" brought smiles to faces.

And there were lots of other boats, mostly snowbirds like us, heading for the Hudson with their masts on their decks. There was *Lady Ann* from Grand Rapids, with a five-year plan to cruise the Mediterranean, and *Early Out,* heading for Boston. We played leapfrog with these and others on their way to the Bahamas, Florida, and the Caribbean all the way across to the Hudson. We began to experience the camaraderie that exists among cruising people.

(Actually, we only had one snowbird [a person cruising south to avoid the northern winter] on board—me. Margaret loves snow and cold, and I doubt that Pukka, an indoor cat, is much aware of seasonal changes.)

There were also the pseudo canal boats chartered by vacationers. Built to look like the old mule-drawn boats, they have nice accommodations and come complete with diesel engines and bikes on the roof. We came across a family reunion of folks from Wyoming and Colorado in a flotilla of three or four of these pretty craft.

In western New York, the canal is a man-made cut crossing flat open country. In one long stretch it is elevated 60 feet, so that when you catch a glimpse through the trees which line the edges, you get a distant view of the surrounding farmland. In one instance, the canal actually crosses *over* a road. In the eastern part of the state, however, the countryside is hilly and much of the canal runs through canalized rivers.

More on Locks and Other Diversions

WE TIED UP AT LOCK 20 one night, between Rome and Utica, and were entertained by a country music program going on in a pavilion tucked in under the pine trees. Lock 20 is also the home of *Betsy,* a former canal

A charter canal boat tied up at Pittsford, left. Right, snowbirds docked at Brockport for the night, *Witch of Endor* on the left.

Left, the upper pool of Lock 20. Right, lock 20 has a regular spectator's gallery. When the townsfolk gather to watch, boaters locking through are literally "on deck"!

work barge which is dressed up with a stage, flags and flower tubs. She was taking the night off when we were there, but she usually is traveling up and down the canal, visiting canal parks and canal towns with all sorts of shows and concerts during summertime Canal Days events.

At St. Johnsville we stayed at the Municipal Marina, which is situated in a little indentation off the canal, next to the Town Park. There was a big concert and picnic in progress, with live bluegrass music coming from the gazebo, and families were gathered at picnic tables and lounging on lawn chairs and blankets. The concert was sponsored by the National Endowment for the Arts.

I guess cats enjoy bluegrass music—Pukka came on deck to sit in the cockpit and listen. She wore her harness and leash; when on deck she was tethered to a cleat or winch. This was not so much to prevent her from going overboard into the water (a catastrophe that never happened), as it was to deter her from jumping ship when we are tied up to a dock. (Cats just don't seem to know when they're having fun).

Lyons is a pretty canal town, with a Post Office, drug store, and supermarket all within 2 to 4 blocks of the canal. We picked up our first mail drop at the Post Office, and it went off without a hitch. We had arranged that Stewart and Ellen would send us a package there, and it was waiting for us. "Oh, you're the boat people", they said. Cute.

Another place we spent the night was Fonda Terminal, which is in the boondocks of Montgomery County. There is absolutely nothing there in the way of services, not even cleats to tie to—just huge bollards spaced about one hundred and twenty feet apart on the concrete bulkhead. I was *very* glad to have those 80-foot dock lines on board! (Pre-departure advice in the Erie Canal literature had said to have four 100-foot dock lines on board. A hundred feet of ½" line is a *huge* bundle—I compromised on 80 feet). The terminal is part of a State maintenance facility, so the grass was mowed, and there was a little bed of flowers for transient boaters to enjoy. But it was the Mohawk Valley Volunteer Fire Department that made this stop memorable.

It was a stunningly beautiful summertime late afternoon. Margaret was below fixing us some supper, and Pukka and I were on deck enjoying the sunshine playing on the hills and water and clouds. I became aware of some commotion up ahead, and upon going on shore to investigate, I saw several pieces of fire fighting equipment, including a big red pumper. Just then the firefighters

Left, Pukka enjoys the bluegrass concert at St. Johnsville. Right, the bridge and lock at Lyons. Downtown and the Post Office are a couple of blocks to the right, and a McDonald's, a supermarket, and a drugstore are on the left side of the canal, an easy walk over the bridge.

Witch of Endor tied up at one of the few eastbound "up" locks on the canal, needed to lock over the Mohawk Mountains. The doors are open. When you motor into an upbound lock and the heavy steel doors close behind you, it is like being at the bottom of a dank, slimy well.

turned that thing on, directing enormous streams of sparkling water arching high into the golden sunlight over the canal. It was an awesome sight.

It seems that the Fire Department does this every two or three weeks for practice and to test their equipment. Think about it . . . . these guys get to come out every couple of weeks and have fun playing with their toys!

From the Newsletter, August 2: Here's How We Locked Through

A S THIS IS WRITTEN, we are in the Hudson River, and our locking experiences are behind us for now, but I want to tell you about how we did the locks.

The water level of Lake Erie is 570 feet above the water level of the Hudson River, which is essentially at sea level. As we traveled east across New York State, the locks lowered us that distance. (By comparison, the Panama Canal deals with a difference in elevation of 85 feet.) The amount of drop at each lock varies from six to 40 feet; typically, they are 12 to 25 feet. Going east, then, they are all going down, except for three, which go up in order to get over the Mohawk Mountains. Locking down is much easier than locking up, because water leaving a lock causes a lot less turbulence in the lock than water entering a lock.

What happens is that you call the lock tender on channel 13 as you approach to let him (or her) know that you are there, and that would like to lock through. The steel gates may be standing open with the green light on; if so, you go right in. If the gates are closed with the red light on, you just stand out there, or circle, or tie up on the wall, depending on conditions and how long its going to be before the lock is ready for you.

Once inside, you head for the starboard wall and pick up the thick, slimy lines (gloves are a necessity) which hang down the lock wall every 15 feet or so, one for the bow and one for the stern. Margaret did the bow, so as I brought the boat gradually to a near stop on the wall, she would be at the bow picking up a line with a boat hook to serve as the stern line, passing it back to me. I would put the engine in neutral, and climb out of the cockpit to the side deck to take the line from her boat hook, and she would then pick up another line to be the bow line.

We then were positioned bow and stern, each holding a line in one hand and a strong pole like a boat hook in the other. This was usually accomplished with only minor screaming at each other, much to the disappointment of the watching townsfolk—after all, they came out to the lock to be entertained.

After the gates close behind you, the lock keeper opens the valves to lower the water level in the lock, and the boat begins to move down. This causes some turbulence, and you prevent the boat from moving either into or too far away from the slimy wall by paying out the line with one hand, while fending off the wall

A downbound motor cruiser entering and leaving a lock.

with the pole in the other. It can be a bit of a chore to prevent the water turbulence from pushing the boat against the rough wall as it moves downward. Fenders and fenderboards are of course a necessity. We just kept ours in place the entire time we were on the canal.

When the water is finished leaving the lock, you are at the bottom of a dank, slimy well. When the huge steel lock doors open in front of you, you push off the wall and motor out into the sunshine, having achieved another 20 feet or so of vertical travel down to sea level.

The Waterford Flight

THE ERIE CANAL lets you go with a bang. It's final hug and kiss as you descend to sea level at Waterford, where the canal joins the Hudson, is the "Flight of Five"— five locks in a mile and a half that let you down the final 169 feet. This is *very* busy two hours. These locks are so close to each other that the lower pool of one is the upper pool of the next, so you don't have the usual respite afforded by motoring for a spell to the next lock. But we did just fine. *Endor* is our name and survival is our game.

Happily, I did not at the time think about the fact that on the way home we would have the much more difficult task of doing this in reverse. Sufficient unto the day is the evil thereof.

2

Hudson River to Chesapeake Bay

Sea Level at Last!

WE SPENT TWO DAYS at the Troy Town Dock on the Hudson, going grocery shopping (using the marina pickup), doing laundry, and picking up a mail package from Stewart and Ellen that had been sent to the marina.

We also had our mast stepped there. Troy Town Dock is a good place to stop for an overnight or for a couple of days—especially if you've come down the Waterford Flight late in the day—but we would not recommend having your mast put up there. It was simply unnecessarily difficult and expensive. There are better options: Castleton-on-Hudson is about 13 miles south, and Catskill is a day's run or about 30 miles down river. The Castleton-on-Hudson Yacht Club, for a modest fee, allows sailors to use its do-it-yourself crane for mast stepping (not my style), and there are a couple of places up Catskill Creek which will step your mast. We made a note to have our mast taken down there on the return trip.

At Troy we prepared for our week's run down the Hudson to the New York City area by putting away all the Erie Canal charts and guides, and getting out the *Waterway Guide Chartbook, New York Waters.* For planning anchorages and marinas on the Hudson, we continued to use the Rumsey book and *Waterway Guide, Northern Edition.*

The Mighty Hudson

THE HUDSON RIVER is a delight. It is a broad and scenic waterway that winds majestically through the Taconic and Catskill Mountains. The fact that we were a sailboat again, sailing and motorsailing in spacious waters with aids to navigation, channels, shoals, and commercial traffic added to our pleasure. As we traveled south, we discovered the historic Hudson River lighthouses, and enjoyed spotting sights such as FDR's home at Hyde Park. We also saw other

Sailing down this river among those magnificent hills was a memorable experience. The visual scale of this place is breathtaking, with fresh panoramas unfolding around each bend. Above, the US Military Academy at West Point nestles on the riverbank; a gaff-rigged sloop sails to windward.

There are several historic lighthouses on the Hudson. This is the Kingston-Rondout lighthouse, which stands at the entrance to Rondout Creek. We spent time on Rondout Creek on both the up and down legs of our cruise, at anchor in its upper reaches and tied up at the Kingston Town Docks. Photo courtesy of Rod Watson.

mansions high on the heavily wooded eastern bank that we recognized, but could not specifically identify; we had seen them on Discovery Channel's *American Castles* series.

Three of the six nights on the Hudson between Troy and Tarrytown at the Tappan Zee Bridge were spent at anchor: Esopus Creek at Saugerties, Low Point at Chelsea, and Verplanck Point just below Peekskill. Chelsea and Verplanck were fine; Esopus Creek was not good.

Walter (at the time of our cruise, Walter Cronkite was prominently associated with the *Waterway Guide* series, and throughout the trip we simply referred to the books as "Walter". This enabled us to blame poor Walter for our bad choices)—Walter calls the anchorage "cozy and attractive". I would call it too small and attractive. It simply was not big enough for a 30' boat to set or swing to an anchor, particularly when there are a couple of other boats in there. But we did indeed find it attractive by moonlight, when we were aroused during the night, gently bumping against a dock.

Our afternoon at Catskill Marina was marked by a pleasant swim in the pool and the purchase of a new Hudson River chart. The Hudson part of the *Chartbook* was out of date—buoys had been re-numbered. There is nothing quite as disconcerting in unfamiliar waters as

The anchoring spot up Esopus Creek was pretty but small.

finding that the buoys and navigation aids shown on the chart are different from what you are actually seeing out on the water.

The time we spent at the town docks on pretty Rondout Creek was memorable. Rondout Creek is the old harbor for Kingston, and it is a most agreeable place. You tie up at a shady park in the restored waterfront district, which features a variety of boutiques for window (if not actual) shopping, and three or four good restaurants. There is also the Hudson River Maritime Center Museum, which is well worth a visit.

We looked for a barbershop because I was beginning to need a haircut. It seemed strange that we didn't find one—until we looked around and saw that every man in sight was either bald or had hair to his shoulders.

The question of whether to dine at the Chinese restaurant or the Japanese restaurant was a major one for me, because I am fond of both cuisines. I thought about it a lot as we worked up an appetite while perusing the museum. I finally decided on Chinese, with the resolution to stop at Roundout again next year on the way home for the Japanese restaurant. (I was close to having a Chinese food deprivation attack. This is a serious matter with me.

On the Erie Canal I was looking forward to stopping at Cooper's Marina near Baldwinsville, because the Rumseys say in *A Cruising Guide to the Northeast's Waterways* that there is a Chinese restaurant across the street. As soon as we were tied up at Coopers, I ran to look across the street, and it had been turned into a pizzeria . . . a *pizzeria!* I had been anticipating that meal since before we left Sandusky. While this is not cause to pan the Rumsey book, it comes close. Reasonableness has no place where Chinese food is involved. We did have an excellent meal at another restaurant down the road, but . . . . . there are scars).

Passing the US Military Academy at West Point was another highlight. I got very excited as we approached it and I went through a lot of videotape as we sailed by. But it takes a long time to get past, and it was not until we reached its southern end that I realized that *here* was the famous shot of West Point—the massive stone battlements rising from the water's edge, capped by soaring gothic structures. I had just created a festoon of fascinating footage featuring such famous attractions as the West Point field house, power plant, and laundry. Oh well.

When we got down to Tarrytown, which is just north of New York City, we hunkered down for a night at the Tarrytown Marina next to the Tappan Zee Bridge. We put on our backpacks, walked to the supermarket for some grocery shopping, and later stocked up on fuel and ice to be ready for the next day's adventure. The next night would be spent below Manhattan on Staten Island, where we planned to visit with college friends.

New York, New York, it's a Wonderful Town

THE BRONX IS UP and the Battery's down! Now things were *really* getting exciting. Margaret and I are both Easterners—I was born in mid-town Manhattan and grew up in suburban New York, and Margaret was raised in Stamford, Connecticut. The idea of our cruising down the

Hudson in our own sailboat. . past Morningside Heights with Grant's Tomb and Riverside Church . . Mid-town and 42nd Street . . The Empire State Building . . the Battery . . The Statute of Liberty . . and out under the Verrazano-Narrows Bridge . . was simply <u>not</u> believable. If you had told me 40 years ago that I would be doing this, I would have asked you what you were smoking, because I would have wanted some too.

We did it all the next day—and the actual event far exceeded the expectation. This was one of the most exciting days of my life. Who would have ever thought that this stodgy couple—just plain Ohio folks—having set out from Sandusky in their little boat, would be sailing down New York Harbor, past the Statute of Liberty and the anchored shipping, out through The Narrows and Lower Bay, dodging the inbound and outbound container ships in the Ambrose Channel, and into the open Atlantic beyond?

We pass a northbound tug and barge under the George Washington Bridge.

Margaret at the helm in New York Harbor, with the skyline of downtown Manhattan in the background, dominated by the World Trade Center towers. She's taking us past Miss Liberty, right.

Well, not quite. Actually, we were scheduled to visit friends on Staten Island, and needed to stop at Great Kills Harbor in the Lower Bay, on Staten Island's eastern shore. We had difficulty finding Great Kills, which was stupid because we had GPS on board. (Global Positioning System—a device that bounces signals off of satellites and tells you where you are and the compass heading to steer to get to where you want to go). We had become so accustomed to traveling in canals and rivers that we just forgot all about it.

The Lower Bay has some significant shoals, especially near the entrance to Great Kills, so it was a stressful time. The difficulty in these situations is trying to figure out whether the lighthouse, or buoy, or other navigation aid that you are looking at is the one you think it is on the chart; or, to put it plainly, just trying to figure out where the hell you are. If you don't know your location on the chart, you could at any moment hit a rocky shoal.

Fear is never far from the surface in cruising, at least in my experience. For me there is a hierarchy of stressful situations, beginning with going aground in sand or

We head for the Verrazano-Narrows Bridge on our way out of New York Harbor to the Lower Bay and Great Kills Harbor on Staten Island.

mud (not bad—you can usually get off without help and damage is unlikely), which would be a level one. Danger of hitting rocks would be a level four or five. Entering an unfamiliar marina with wind and current, uncertain water depth, and uncertainty about the layout and where to go, can be a level two or three. The most stressful events are those related to weather—violent weather can be life threatening. Like many sailors (I think), my respect for weather and water can quickly turn to fear.

So, anxiety and stomach-churning apprehension are always near, and the remedy is to maintain confidence in yourself and in your boat and its equipment, and to never allow fear to control your actions. Deep breathing also helps. It gets oxygen to the brain, which at my age needs all the help it can get. There is also much to be said for having a St. Christopher medallion on board.

The pay-off is in the challenge and excitement of mastering anxieties, in the sense of accomplishment and total relaxation when you arrive and are securely tied to a dock, and in the sheer enjoyment of being on the water.

Anyway, we proceeded with caution, enjoyed a little luck, and made it safely into Great Kills Harbor. Remember: *Endor* is our name and survival is our game.

Home in the Atlantic

A FTER A WONDERFUL VISIT of several days with our good friends, we sailed across the Lower Bay, rounded Sandy Hook, and proceeded off-shore down the coast of New Jersey.

Now, this was an event of consequence for the *Witch of Endor.* Her namesake was a 10-gun Cutter of the Royal Navy during the Napoleonic Wars, whose home was the Atlantic Ocean. Our *Witch* was built in France and transported to Cleveland on the deck of a freighter; the only water she knew up until very recently was the fresh water of the Great Lakes, 570 feet up. So she was one happy little boat that day, romping down the Jersey coast in her ancestral waters. I grew up on the Atlantic, and I was pleased also, but I did not romp.

Many sailors take the New Jersey coast as a continuous all day/night run down to Cape May. It's a little more than 100 miles. We are day sailors, and we found that the trip breaks easily into three days, coming inside at night. There are a number of inlets, and many of them are dangerous. The ones we used are safe, easy, and conveniently spaced: Manasquan Inlet, Atlantic City, and Cape May.

There are buoys one to three miles off shore all the way down the coast. With a little planning, and by entering some of these as waypoints in the GPS, we always knew what course to steer and how long it was going to take to get to our destination. We watched the weather, checking the forecast each day; the weather held wonderfully, and the result was three days of great sailing down the coast.

We came inside at the Manasquan Inlet, entered the Point Pleasant Canal, and worked our way down the New Jersey Intracoastal, inside the barrier islands, for a short distance. We were due to visit friends at their summer place in Mantolocking Shores.

At the helm off the New Jersey coast—the weather held and we had three days of great sailing. Right, *Witch of Endor* tied up at Harrah's in Atlantic City.

The short (thank God!) Point Pleasant Canal provided us with our first experience with *very* strong current. We were going against the current, which is good. Although it means slower going, you have much better control of the boat when going against the current. But we got too close to the side, and the current pinned the boat against the corrugated steel bulkhead.

Now, a boat changes direction by swinging the stern to one side or the other while moving ahead. So the only way we could get off was by steering toward the center of the canal while powering hard, which pushed the stern hard against the corrugated steel bulkhead. After some severe scraping, we managed to get off. This was not so much a fearful situation as it was a how to destroy the side of your boat situation. Oh well. I can to this day reflect on the dangers of strong currents in bulkheaded canals by going out to the marina and gazing morosely at the small area of damage that remains. Great Lakes sailors have no idea how lucky they are not to have to deal with tides and tidal currents.

We also went aground in the mud a few times back in there. All in all, not a good day, but soon we were snugly moored at the dock behind our friends' house.

These are college friends, and they had arranged for a mini-reunion of our old crowd (we're talking the 1950's here), including a couple who flew in from Seattle. What a blast! We ate like animals for two days, and just had a marvelous time. There are no friends like old friends, especially old friends with a dock behind their house.

Continuing down the Jersey coast, we came in at Atlantic City, where we spent the night tied up at Harrah's Marina. We did not gamble, but boy did we eat—Harrah's has an incredible buffet.

We came in again at Cape May, where we stayed a couple days, both anchored in the harbor near the Coast Guard Station, and at a marina. Cape May looked like an interesting place to spend some time to explore, and we vowed to do so on the way home.

On to the Chesapeake!

T HE CAPE MAY CANAL is a three mile cut that takes you westward across the southern tip of the barrier island to the bottom of Delaware Bay. This eliminates what I understand can be an uncomfortable trip outside around Cape May Point. It is also a lot quicker.

As we headed up Delaware Bay towards the Delaware River and the C & D Canal entrance, the bay lived up to its nasty reputation, and we battled severe rainstorms with high winds and heavy seas most of the day. (We should never have left Cape May—the weather signs were all there—you just never learn). Our destination was the Cohansey River, on the Jersey side about 38 miles up

Tied up at Mantolocking Shores. Party time again!

bay where it becomes the Delaware River. We were in our foul weather gear, and were harnessed and tethered to the boat. After six and half hours of dodging container ships and barge tows in very uncomfortable conditions, the weather cleared, and we anchored peacefully in golden afternoon sunlight in the Cohansey River. Except for occasional fishing boats passing by, this was a beautifully secluded spot. We lost an anchor that night, however. It is a narrow place to anchor, and a passing boat probably cut the line.

(The trip up Delaware Bay that day was not particularly stressful—we had no doubts about the boat or ourselves—it was simply *extremely* uncomfortable.)

The C & D (Chesapeake and Delaware) is a 15 mile big ship canal which connects the Delaware River just south of Wilmington, with the Elk River at the top of Chesapeake Bay. We had an uneventful passage through the C & D, spending the night tied up at Schaeffer's Canal House, which is most of the way across the canal at Chesapeake City, Maryland. The current in the canal is fierce and in the process of getting away from the bulkhead at Schaeffer's, we banged the GPS antennae, which is mounted on the stern rail, damaging its innards.

Speaking of damaged innards, Schaeffer's sells their own brand of liquor _really_ cheap. I'm talking five or six dollars a bottle. Liquor everywhere in Maryland is very inexpensive, but this was crazy. I bought some vodka and whiskey (yeah, just "Whiskey") for ship's stores. We'll see. (I am still alive. My head does twitch around a bit, but I always did have this vacant stare. It is the drool that has me worried).

We spent a day at anchor in a cove on the Elk River not far from Chesapeake City, because of heavy rain and poor visibility. Margaret spent the day knitting, Pukka snoozed (working hard at her daily 26 hours), and I had the floorboards up trying to locate and fix a

Witch of Endor docked at Schaeffer's Canal House on the C&D Canal. The C&D is always busy with big ship traffic. Freighters headed for Wilmington and Philadelphia travel up the Chesapeake and transit the C&D to reach the Delaware River. They are required to have pilots on board while in US inland waters, and Schaeffer's is the transfer point for Maryland and Delaware pilots. The ship in the background has just dropped off its Maryland pilot and picked up its Delaware pilot. The ship does not stop—a little pilot boat goes out from the dock and runs along beside the freighter, maintaining the same speed, while the pilots climb up and down a ladder hanging over the side.

problem we began to have on the Hudson: the fresh water tanks were emptying into the bilge.

Havre de Grace, Maryland

OUR FIRST PORT OF CALL in the Chesapeake was Havre de Grace. We had a five day layover there for provisioning, getting a haircut (the haircut situation had become a crisis), and picking up mail. We also needed some time for boatkeeping chores like replacing the GPS antenna (had to be shipped from the manufacturer), solving and getting the plumbing problem fixed, and replacing the lost anchor and line.

We stayed at the friendly and professional Tidewater Marina, which is also a full service boat yard.

This marina has an unusually well stocked ship's store, and the marina personnel were helpful in getting our boat problems sorted out and fixed.

Havre de Grace is at the very top of Chesapeake Bay, where the Susquehanna River flows into the Bay. The Susquehanna begins in Otsego Lake, New York, and meanders for 438 miles through forests, farmlands, mountains, and valleys, and pours 24 billion gallons of fresh water into the Chesapeake each day. This is almost 50% of the Bay's fresh water intake.

We liked Havre de Grace a lot. It has an old fashioned downtown, complete with a 5 and 10 cent store, ice cream parlors, and the Chat 'n Chew Cafe. We had our first Maryland crab cakes of the trip, climbed the lighthouse, visited museums and other attractions, and thoroughly enjoyed our visit. We also had a healthy 5-mile round trip walk to the Post Office to pick up our mail package. The Post Office had been moved from the downtown building near the marina (the reason I arranged this particular mail drop) to a spanking new building in an outlying area.

The New York and other northern charts and guides were retired and we switched to Chesapeake Bay materials for planning and navigating. These included the Mid-Atlantic edition of Walter's *Waterway Guide*, and Chesapeake Bay Magazine's *Charts of the Chesapeake*, with its companion, *Guide to Cruising Chesapeake Bay*. We also had on board *Cruising the Chesapeake* by Shellenberger, published by International Marine.

Two other resources which we used for the balance of the trip deserve mention: the *Intracoastal Waterway Facilities Guide*, which contains useful information about marinas, and International Marine's *Light List and Waypoint Guide,* compiled by the Kettlewells. It provides the coordinates of buoys and navigation aids from Maine to Texas—useful for entering waypoints into the GPS.

From the Newsletter, August 27: Miscellany

WE ARE WRITING THIS on the laptop, sitting under the cockpit awning while swinging gently to our anchor behind an island on the Sassafras River in the upper Chesapeake. It is late in the day. The trees are black paper silhouettes against the yellow, red, and purple western sky. Waterfowl swim silently, fanning iridescent V-ripples across the still pond. Pukka joins us in the cockpit and watches them with feline intensity. Ice rustles in a glass of Schaeffer's rotgut and water; Mozart gentles the air.

My friends, I must tell you . . . it just does not get any better than this. We will spend time in the Chesapeake. Tomorrow, after checking out Georgetown, up the Sassafras, we will head down-Bay. Our plans for the coming weeks include visiting Baltimore's inner harbor, stopping at various ports down the fabled Eastern Shore, and sailing up the Potomac River. We plan to anchor in the

Are we there yet?

shadow of the Washington monument for a week, visiting with our son and daughter-in-law, Kerry and Joann, who live in suburban DC.

For our animal loving friends, Pukka the sea kitty is doing well. She sometimes keeps Margaret awake at night by batting her toys around. She has yet to perform any useful work around the boat—a matter of growing concern for me.

Another note, to give credit where it is due: because of the references in these newsletters to great eating off the boat, the reader may have gained the impression that meals aboard the boat are lacking in some way. AU CONTRAIRE! Margaret is doing an incredible job in her little galley, and meals on board run the gamut from super to superb.

3

Chesapeake Bay

A Place of Contrasts

THE WEEKS THAT WE SPENT in the Chesapeake were just delightful. The time was too short; to really explore this marvelous place would take years. Visualizing a map of the Bay, it describes a sinuous double curve, narrow at the top and a bit wider as it nears the Atlantic. Its wonder lies in the many rivers that flow down into it on each side, each with its own system of meandering streams and creeks waiting to be explored, hiding towns and hamlets waiting to be discovered. When the wind is right, sailing on the Bay is terrific, but you need to pay close attention to the charts and aids to navigation because of the many shoal areas. We had some great sailing, some nice motorsailing, and a lot of motoring.

For us, the Chesapeake contrasted big city excitement with small town serenity and quiet anchorages. We spent part of Labor Day weekend anchored in Baltimore's inner harbor, an intimate place surrounded by office towers, hotels, museums, shops, and restaurants. On holiday weekends, the shore esplanade and plazas surrounding the harbor are crowded with street entertainers and tourists. Water taxis, tour boats, and a profusion of petite pedal craft complete the festive holiday scene. It was such fun to be in

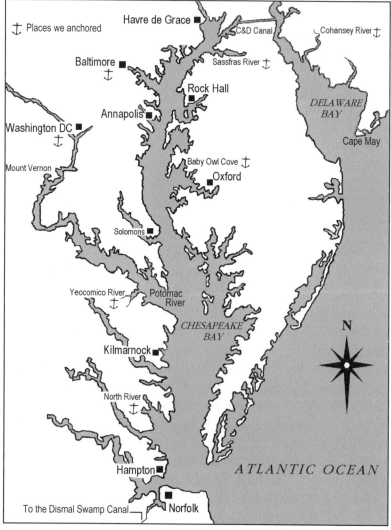

Map of Chesapeake Bay, showing Cape May, Delaware Bay, and the C&D Canal.

Baltimore's inner Harbor, Labor Day weekend. *Witch of Endor* at far right.

the middle of all this! And the harbor was not crowded—
there were only four or five other boats anchored there.

Rocking gently at anchor, we dined under our
awning in the cockpit with candlelight and crystal (plastic
wineglasses), providing a diversion for the peacefully
pedaling Baltimoreans.

We rowed our dinghy to the dinghy dock each
day for sightseeing. A highlight of our stay was the water
taxi ride to tour Fort McHenry. It guards the entrance to
Baltimore Harbor, and it was the site of:

> *". . . . the rockets' red glare,*
> *the bombs bursting in air,*
> *gave proof through the night*
> *that our Flag was still there!"*

Francis Scott Key wrote that lyric during the war
of 1812, while observing the British attack on Fort McHenry
from the deck of a British warship, where he was being
held prisoner. The flag which flies over this fort is (and was)

huge. The original is on display at the Smithsonian in DC. It is impressive.

We also enjoyed touring the USCGC *Willow*, a brand new Coast Guard buoy tender that was tied up right there in the inner harbor for public inspection. Her bridge was loaded with the latest electronic gear. We observed her unmooring and departure, and were amused at the process. The crew member left on the shore to cast off the huge bow and stern lines was a little girl Coastie who looked about sixteen and at 5'-4" probably weighed 102 pounds.

She released the stern line first and then, head down and arms pumping, raced forward to the bollard holding the bow line, dodging tourist families and strollers like a broken field runner. She released the bow line and with the big cutter, its engine rumbling, drifting off the dock and beginning to move out into the harbor, she ran back amidships to where buoy tenders are cut low and took a flying leap into the brawny arms of her crewmates,

The Coast Guard Cutter *Willow* docked in Baltimore's inner harbor. *Witch of Endor* is anchored in the foreground.

The Thomas Point Shoal light is a
Chesapeake landmark.

who pulled her on board.

I guess she has this job because she is the swiftest, and the easiest to haul on board. It was charming. I wonder how many times she has been left behind!

The Eastern Shore

BY WAY OF CONTRAST, we spent a quiet week in the Eastern Shore town of Oxford on the Tred Avon River, which is a tributary of the Choptank River. This is the locale of James A. Michener's wonderful epic novel, *Chesapeake,* which I enjoyed reading while preparing for the cruise.

Oxford epitomizes the Eastern Shore. First settled in 1683, it is small, green, and bordered on three sides by water. Marinas full of workboats (oyster and crab boats) and sailboats crowd Town Creek. Oxford is not a tourist attraction like nearby St. Michaels, which is busy and full of trendy shops and yachties. It is a peaceful place of nicely restored and maintained houses on tree shaded roads and lanes with brick sidewalks. You can see the water from practically everywhere. Oxford is quietly and genuinely stylish—simply a beautiful place, world class in every respect.

We stayed at Crockett Brothers, an excellent full service marina and boatyard with a good selection of Yanmar® spare parts in their store. (Yanmar is a maker of sailboat diesel engines). This yard did a good job replacing the electric heating element in our hot water heater.

Kerry and Joann visited with us for a weekend in Oxford, and we went on a mini-cruise up nearby Broad Creek and anchored overnight in Baby Owl Cove.

We also spent a couple of days at the Eastern Shore town of Rock Hall, where we had a great seafood dinner, picked up a mail package, and stocked up with more cheap Maryland liquor. We met a couple there who sold their house and moved aboard their boat when their kids started moving back in their home, bringing *their* kids.

Inside the Beltway

OUR CRUISE UP THE POTOMAC to Washington, DC was the highlight of our Chesapeake experience. The Potomac is wide and meandering with many tributaries and places to explore on both the Maryland and Virginia sides. The final day of the trip up the river was exciting as we passed Mt. Vernon and, rounding the last bend, sighted the Washington monument and the Capitol dome in the distance.

There was, however, a significant obstacle lying between us and the delights of the Capitol City: the Woodrow Wilson Bridge, where I-495 (the Beltway) crosses the Potomac at Alexandria, VA. This bridge is supposed to have 50 feet of clearance between the surface of the water and its underside. The top of *Witch of Endor's* mast (including antennae and wind direction indicator), is about 48 feet above the water's surface.

Well, you say, there's 50 feet of clearance and you only need 48 feet, so what's the problem? Well, *I* say, whadduya mean, what's the problem? —that's *too close!*

We found it! It's at Rock Hall, Maryland.

How do I know that the bridge is *really* 50 feet up? It looks more like 47 feet to me! It's the skipper's job to be paranoid about his $20,000 rig being wiped out by a damn bridge! Do you think Woodrow Wilson is going to pay for a new mast?

The bridge does open, but only between 12 midnight and five AM, and then only if you give them 12 hour's notice by telephone. *You have to call to make an appointment to get through the damn bridge in the middle of the night!* And then, there you would be—in total darkness in an unfamiliar place surrounded by the lights of Alexandria, Washington National Airport, Bolling Air Force Base, and the District of Columbia, trying to follow a channel marked with unlighted buoys! When I said that I had the skills required for coastal cruising, this is *not* what I had in mind.

What we did was to time ourselves to arrive at the bridge at low tide, which on that day was 3:30 in the afternoon. (Margaret was in charge of tides. She was equipped with a marvelous hand-held device called Tidetracker®, which enabled her to predict the time of high, low or slack tide just about anyplace on the Eastern seaboard). I will never forget this. We inched our way under, and I mean *inched,* with less than a half knot showing on the knotmeter. My heart was thumping and my hand was on the backstay to feel that first touch, which I *knew* would come, while the mate offered quiet words of comfort like, ". . . it'll only take off the top few inches . . ."

At anchor in D.C.'s Washington Channel.

Well, we made it. Actually, there was plenty of clearance. The problem is that when you are approaching a bridge, and looking up at the bridge and up at the top of your mast, the bridge can be 80 feet and your mast 40 feet, and it still looks as if you are going to hit. It is a well-known phenomenon of perspective known as "Sailor's Paranoia".

Approaching the anchorage in what is known as the Washington Channel was a happy and exciting experience for me. Thirty years of business travel in and out of Washington National Airport, US Army time spent at Ft. Meyer and Ft. McNair some years before that, and my parents having lived in the District in the 50's and 60's, combine to give me a sense of having roots in Washington. This sense is now heightened by Kerry and Joann's living and working in the area. Motoring slowly past the airport, and past the Army War College and Ft. McNair to the anchorage, was a high I will not soon forget.

Anchored in the Shadow

WE SPENT A MARVELOUS WEEK anchored there, living aboard our boat literally in the shadow of the Washington monument. Twenty-five dollars a week to the Gangplank Marina, which borders the anchorage, provided us with a secure dock for the dinghy a short distance away from our boat, and also access to showers restrooms, and laundry facilities. (This marina is the home of a large live-aboard population, including at that time US Representative James Traficant, Congressman from Youngstown, Ohio).

The picture of the Washington monument, above, was taken from *Witch of Endor's* cockpit. The picture of the Washington channel, below, was taken from the top of the monument. *Witch of Endor* is one of the anchored boats.

Helicopters flew low overhead along the length of the narrow channel at least once a day— probably ferrying our poor, deprived civil servants between the Pentagon, the White House, and Glen Burnie Country Club.

We felt as if we were in the center of everything Washington had to offer. The shore on one side was a landscaped esplanade bordered by the marina, seafood restaurants, markets, and the other side was a large park. A supermarket, a drug store, fast food restaurants, a Chinese restaurant (yea!) and a Metro station were two blocks away. The Washington Mall (Washington Monument, The Smithsonian, the National Gallery, and all the other great Mall attractions) was within an easy walk. L'enfant Plaza (office buildings connected by an underground shopping mall) was also near.

This is a perfect place for cruising boaters to stay in Washington, and we had an outstanding week sightseeing and visiting with Kerry and Joann.

Porpoises in the Potomac

WENDING OUR WAY back down the Potomac to Chesapeake Bay (The District of Columbia lies about three easy days from the Bay), we spent a late afternoon and evening at anchor in a cove up the Yeocomico River, on the Virginia side near the broad mouth of the Potomac. We had stayed there on the way up, and we returned because it is such a lovely spot, wooded and tranquil, with a few houses nestled among the trees. The cove is perhaps 300 feet across, and we were tucked well inside in about seven feet of water. During the evening two or three other boats joined us.

In the morning, as we were moving about on deck taking the awning down, the sail cover off, and doing the chores preparatory to raising the anchor and getting under way, we were visited by a pod of porpoises. There were at least four of them. I saw three out in the Yeocomico, moving (porpoising) slowly down stream toward the Potomac, and one was cavorting near us in the cove, checking us out. We heard the distinctive clicking sound that porpoises make. As we got under way, they stayed near us for a while as we headed out into the Potomac, and then we lost them. We were excited about this—they were the first porpoises we saw, and we did not expect to see them this far north.

From the Newsletter, September 28: We Need to Move On

SEPTEMBER IS DRAWING to a close, and we will soon be leaving the Chesapeake and entering a new phase of our cruise, as we enter the Intracoastal Waterway below Norfolk and travel through coastal North and South Carolina and Georgia on our way to . . . *Florida!*

(Crossing the State line into Florida had become a goal for us. Articles about the Intracoastal Waterway in the boating magazines always mentioned that in Fernandina Beach, the first Florida stop just over the State line, there was a welcome center where cruisers were given a glass of freshly squeezed orange juice. We were looking forward to this.)

We are finishing this newsletter while tied up at the Chesapeake Boat Basin, a small marina at the head of Indian Creek on the Virginia side of the Bay, near the town of Kilmarnock. We have been snuggled into this pretty, wooded place for several days, waiting for heavy weather out on the Bay to subside. We are two days north of Hampton Roads and Norfolk, the door out of the Chesapeake.

Actually, the weather here is beautiful: blue sky, nice breeze. The problem is that a nice breeze up here in the woods is a 30-knot gale out on the Bay, three and a half miles away. So, we're cleaning the boat, finishing this newsletter for copying and mailing from Hampton, and socializing with the other cruising folks tucked into this small world. We also used the marina station wagon for some shopping and a restaurant meal (*fried oysters!*) in nearby Kilmarnok.

We left a load of things behind with Kerry and Joann which we will pick up next year on the way home— the mast supports for the Erie Canal, charts and guides for areas north of the Chesapeake, and other junk which won't be needed until we're heading north again. No point in carrying it to the Keys and back.

From the Newsletter, September 28: Some Chesapeake Highlights

BEST DEAL: Shymansky's Marina and Restaurant, behind Cobb Island on the Maryland side of the Potomac: $15 per night for dockage with water and power, and a sublime fried seafood dinner with soft shell crab, scallops, clams, oysters, and sea bass also $15.

MOST EMBARRASSING MOMENT: at a marina in Galesville, VA, when I dumped used engine oil into a container meant to receive *containers* of used engine oil.

MARGARET tackled half-dozen steamed crabs at Oxford, and did well. I love crab, but that's too much work for me.

PUKKA the sea kitty continues to prosper. She has *finally* begun to earn her keep by catching flies (and eating them—she chomps 'em right down!).

4

North Carolina

From the Newsletter, October 26: Weather Again

RAIN, RAIN, RAIN. We are holed up on Bald Head Island because of rain and poor visibility brought on by a Nor'easter. We could do a lot worse—the Bald Head Island marina, a pretty place at the mouth of the Cape Fear River near Wilmington, North Carolina, is pleasant and inexpensive. It is an opportunity to catch up with boatkeeping and bookkeeping chores and also a chance to work on this newsletter, which is not a chore. In fact, it is pleasant, even in this drizzle, to work on the computer at the cockpit table under the awning, listening to NPR's *Weekend Edition*, and looking around at the other boats docked here.

It is Sunday, and we are anticipating the final game of the World Series tonight. Margaret is below baking cookies. We are looking forward to a pleasant shore dinner tonight at one of the restaurants here at Bald Head. Last night, Margaret fixed baked chicken with mashed potatoes and gravy, and tonight she deserves a rest.

Chesapeake Adieu

BUT I NEED TO BACK UP to where I left off in the last newsletter, when we were on our way out of the Chesapeake at the end of September.

When the high winds subsided, we ventured out of Indian Creek and motorsailed down the Bay towards the entrance to Hampton Roads and Norfolk Harbor. We spent our last Chesapeake night at anchor in a very pretty area up the East River, near the bottom of the Bay on the Virginia side. When considering places to anchor overnight in the Chesapeake you need to allow enough time to get there. The prettiest and most sheltered places are generally well off the beaten track, up the rivers and creeks. This spot was about seven nautical miles from the open waters of the Bay, which is well over an hour each way.

To get there, we went into Mobjack Bay and up the winding East River through wooded country, past nice houses and small private marinas. We chose a likely spot at a bend in the river where we could get out of the main channel, and set our anchor in about eight feet of water. Margaret checked the tide and determined that we wouldn't lose more than a foot or two of water during the night.

The golden sunlight made long shadows across the lawns of the waterfront homes as I changed the propane tank and Margaret fixed a simple supper. While we dined at the cockpit table under the awning, the river turned to glass, reflecting the brilliance of the sunset and the blackness of the silhouetted trees.

The next day we sailed south across the mouth of the York River, rounded Old Point Comfort, and entered Hampton Roads, which is the northern part of Norfolk Harbor. We tied up at the Hampton Public Piers, a short distance up the Hampton River, and spent a couple of days sightseeing, grocery shopping and getting the last newsletter copied, collated, stapled, stickered, and mailed. In addition, I was also able to stock up on a good brand of heavy-duty diesel engine oil.

Hampton Public Piers is a *very* nice and festive place; Hampton has done a great job with its waterfront. The downtown is nicely restored, and, while quiet, seems viable. The waterfront features an Air and Space Museum, which we visited, and a wonderful carousel, which we rode twice.

All the Chesapeake charts and guides were put away; we would now be using the *Waterway Guide Chartbook, Norfolk to Jacksonville.* We continued with the Mid-Atlantic edition of Walter's *Waterway Guide,* and began to use the truly indispensable cockpit reference for the Intracoastal Waterway, *The Intracoastal Waterway Norfolk to Miami: a Cockpit Cruising Handbook* by Jan and Bill Moeller.

George Did It

I WAS APPREHENSIVE ABOUT getting through the Norfolk-Portsmouth harbor complex because I had never been there, and it is one of the busiest ports in the world. But it turned out to be a piece of cake. It was an exciting morning, motoring past huge container ships underway, tugs and tows, and of course a major US Navy presence. If you enjoy feeling insignificant, motoring a 30 foot sailboat down the western branch of the Elizabeth River past the Norfolk Navy Yard and under the towering sterns of huge naval vessels is a prime experience.

There are two ways to proceed from the Elizabeth River south of Portsmouth to the Intracoastal Waterway. We elected the scenic route, known as the Dismal Swamp Canal. It cuts through a swampy region of southern Virginia and northern North Carolina and brings you to the Pasquotank River, which leads to Albemarle Sound. Together with Turner's Cut at its southern end, it is a straight-as-an-arrow 30-mile land cut traversing wild and pretty country.

It is widely believed that as a young man George Washington performed the original surveying work for this

We spent a night tied up at the North Carolina Welcome Center on the Dismal Swamp Canal.

canal. While there is some question about whether this really happened, there is little doubt that he was involved. He owned a good portion of the land it traversed and was an early supporter of the project.

From the Elizabeth River south of Portsmouth, access to the Dismal Swamp Canal is gained through Deep Creek, a pleasant stream bordering a town of the same name. The story goes that during his surveying work for the canal, George slipped, fell into the creek, and exclaimed, "that is a *deep* creek!" The worshipful locals, mindful of his destiny to become the father of their country, named the creek and their town after this solemn event, enabling them and their successors to boast that "George Washington slipped here".

So, watching our step, we motored the Canal, spending a night at the North Carolina Welcome Center about two thirds of the way through. Highway 17 parallels the Canal and the Welcome Center is located between the highway and the Canal, serving both motorists and boaters. What a neat idea! There is a good dock, with space for three to four boats, grass, flower beds, and very helpful folks in the Center itself.

There are a couple of little locks along the way, but nothing to faze veterans of the Erie. You just need to pay attention to your timing, because they work on a fixed schedule.

Albemarle Sound

THE DISMAL SWAMP CANAL joins the Pasquotank River, a narrow and beautiful waterway which winds south through dense woods and feeds into Albemarle Sound. Elizabeth City, North Carolina is located on the Pasquotank just as it widens out before emptying into the sound.

Elizabeth City may not be the prettiest port of call on the Waterway, but it is without question the most hospitable. When more than four or five boats tie up for the night at the free town docks, Fred Fearing and his friends (The Rose Buddies) greet arriving cruisers with roses for the women, and wine, cheese, and chips for all. This has been going on for years, and is a Waterway tradition.

There were only three or four boats tied up the night we were there, but Fred showed up on his golf cart (donated by Willard Scott after he visited Elizabeth City as NBC weatherman a few years ago), and hosted us all to wine, cheese and chips in his front yard a few blocks away.

Albemarle and Pamlico Sounds are reputed to be treacherous because they are relatively shallow and can quickly build steep waves in a blow. But because our home waters in Lake Erie share this characteristic, we had no problem crossing these inland seas. In fact, these passages provided welcome opportunities turn off the engine and do some sailing.

Sailboats transiting the Dismal Swamp Canal. Photo ICW.NET courtesy US Army Corp of Engineers, Norfolk.

Leaving the Pasquotank River, we enjoyed a pleasant sail across Albemarle Sound and up the wide Alligator River. We joined five or six other sailboats anchored for the night at the head of the Alligator-Pungo Canal. This straight and narrow 21-mile land cut leads to the Pungo

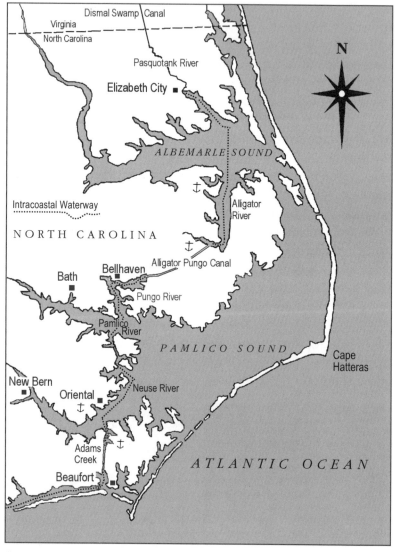

Coastal North Carolina showing Albemarle and Pamlico Sounds and the track of the Intracoastal Waterway.

River which empties into Pamlico Sound. Motoring through these land cuts can be pretty dull. You need to be on the lookout for floating logs, and stay pretty much mid-channel—the edges can be shoal and foul with submerged stumps and debris.

Now that we were traveling the ICW proper (The Intracoastal Waterway technically starts in Norfolk at Mile Zero and ends in Miami at Mile 1,095), we had the benefit of the mile markers. On ICW charts the track of the Waterway is indicated by a solid magenta line. This line is bisected at five-mile intervals by a short, heavier line with numerals representing the cumulative mileage from Mile Zero in Norfolk. Along the Waterway itself, there are actual corresponding mileage signs along the side of the channel. There are sections of the Waterway where these are missing, but they are there most of the way through the Carolinas and Georgia. They are useful. When you don't know what you are doing, you need all the help you can get.

Oyster Fritters!

ONE OF THE PLACES that I was particularly anxious to visit was the River Forest Marina at Belhaven, just off the Pungo River. The reason for this was that the Moellers, in *The Intracoastal Waterway Norfolk to Miami: a Cockpit Cruising Handbook,* say that River Forest serves oyster fritters as part of an outstanding buffet. (You are undoubtedly familiar with the food pyramid which tells you what you're supposed to eat. Well, my personal food pyramid is a little different. It is arranged with the most important foods at the top and stuff like broccoli at the bottom. Fried seafood shares the pinnacle of my pyramid with Chinese food).

Well, we had the oyster fritters, and they were *good.* River Forest Marina is part of River Forest Manor, a handsome Victorian style inn with pretty grounds, tennis courts, and a nice swimming pool (we enjoyed that pool).

Left, the Alligator River Bridge. Right, River Forest Manor in Belhaven. The marina is behind this handsome inn. Photos courtesy of Claiborne S. Young.

Mrs. Axson Smith, a gentle lady whose late husband bought the place 65 years ago, runs the business with some assistance from her sons.

Like the other transient marina in town, River Forest maintains a fleet of electric golf carts for use by their marina guests to go shopping. It was amusing to toodle around downtown in a golf cart, pokin' along through traffic with no direction signals and no brake lights (hardly any brakes)—just hand signals, waves, and smiles. There were a number of them, and I'm sure the police just look the other way (this must be very illegal) because these cruising folks bring a lot of activity to the downtown businesses.

We were at River Forest three days while a mechanic was scheduled to worked on an engine problem (the marina is also a full service boatyard), and it was fun in the afternoons to see those docks fill up with very large motor yachts headed south. The marina would be half empty again by 7:00 AM, but boy, did they pump a lot of gas and diesel through that place. Those big yachts would easily take $300 to $600 worth of fuel, and I'm talking eight to ten of them every day. The underground gas tanks were filled one of the days we were there, and the tank truck driver said that River Forest was one of the largest gas customers in that part of the State. What a revenue stream! To say nothing of all those oyster fritters.

We Explore Coastal North Carolina

THE MANY CREEKS AND RIVERS that flow into Albemarle and Pamlico sounds provide endless possibilities for visiting interesting, out-of-the-way places, very much like the Chesapeake, and we left the track of the Waterway for this purpose several times.

We detoured up the Pamlico River and then Bath Creek to visit Bath, the oldest town in North Carolina. It was the region's first port of entry, and the seat of the first colonial assembly in 1743. In spite of this colorful history, Bath is *very* quiet. By quiet I mean practically no people—the world has passed this place by. While tied up at the State dock, I was able to use my Sun Shower® (a clear plastic bag holding a couple of gallons of water that you fill and heat by leaving it on the deck in the sun) for a shower and shave in the cockpit.

Bath is beautiful. It boasts the oldest church building in the State, St. Thomas', built in 1734. St. Thomas' possesses silver altar service presented to the congregation by King George II, and a church bell given by Queen Anne around 1732. There are also several fully restored eighteenth century houses in Bath. In North Carolina, the work of preserving and presenting historic sites is performed by the State, and it does a great job.

A point of particular interest about Bath is that the novelist Edna Ferber attended a traveling theatrical performance on a boat tied up there, providing the impetus

The State Dock and the restored Palmer-Johnson house in beautiful Bath.
Photos courtesy of Claiborne S. Young.

for her novel *Showboat*, on which the Broadway musical and subsequent movie were based. This is described on an historic marker in the tree-shaded park next to the State dock. This was interesting, because one associates *Showboat* with the Mississippi River. Anyway, we liked Bath. It is a green and tranquil place.

Another town I had heard a lot about and looked forward to visiting was Oriental, at the mouth of the Neuse River off Pamlico Sound. Oriental has a good harbor, with a sheltered anchorage. We stayed at the Oriental Marina, and enjoyed an excellent meal at the adjacent restaurant.

An unusually well-stocked marine store, The Inland Waterway Treasure Company, is located across the street from the marina. It has a large selection of boat hardware, engine spares, clothing, charts, books—you name it, they've got it. I was able to pick up more engine oil for the diesel, an item which is not easy to find. I change the *Witch's* oil after every 100 hours of operation, so I'm always looking for good quality heavy-duty diesel engine oil.

While browsing through the clothing, we saw some lightweight shorts on sale. I'm always looking for nice summer shorts, so we bought a pair. Somewhere on down the line as I was putting them on for the first time, I noticed that they had no pockets. "This is strange", I thought, "why would they make shorts with no pockets?" Then I noticed they had no zipper. "What's this? There's no zipper!" Then I realized that they were boxer shorts. *Underwear!* I don't use that kind, so I didn't recognize them in the store. They have "Oriental" embroidered on them. They are charming. Actually, they have turned out to be just the thing when puttering around the boat, or anchored out someplace. They are cool. I mean *cool*.

We also traveled up the Neuse River to New Bern, North Carolina, and spent five days in this incredibly charming southern city. In contrast to Bath where the State dock was nice, but simply a place to tie up for free

Oriental Marina and Motel, left. Right, we toured the restored Tryon Palace in New Bern, built for the Royal Governor William Tryon, 1767 to 1770. Photos courtesy of Claiborne S. Young.

with zero services (like water, electricity, ice, showers, etc.), in New Bern we stayed at the Sheraton Grand New Bern Marina, part of a large waterside hotel complex, where we enjoyed all first class services as if we were hotel guests. And, it was *not* expensive. (This means $.85 per foot of boat length or $25.50 a night for a 30 foot boat, compared to $1.00 to $2.00 per foot per night, the average being perhaps $1.20) Not bad when you consider the first rate bathroom, shower, and laundry facilities, and free ice.

An aside for non-boating readers: cruising boats of course have more or less complete bathroom facilities but they tend to be cramped, and it is always a pleasure to get ashore for a more spacious ablutive experience. In addition, one seeks opportunities to avoid filling up the holding tank, because getting it pumped out is a pain in the you know where. Of course, one does occasionally find a marina where one is better off making do on board.

The Sheraton Grand Marina is right downtown, and New Bern has much to offer within easy strolling distance—restaurants, ice cream parlors, and interesting historical attractions. New Bern was the first old (dating to the early 1700's) southern city that we visited, and walking through the early residential areas was a delight.

I am at a loss (can you believe it?) to describe the beauty and charm of the houses, the street scenes, and the gardens.

We kept busy during our stay, sightseeing, grocery shopping, dining in a couple of inexpensive restaurants downtown, and visiting the ice cream parlors. We found a small Anglican Church which we enjoyed attending on the Sunday we were there.

New Bern—indeed, much of coastal North Carolina—seems to be full of former Clevelanders. The Indians were in the in the American League playoffs, and we wore Cleveland Indians shirts and caps—always sure conversation-starters. If you are familiar with Cleveland winters you understand why Clevelanders wind up in the Carolinas. (But never Margaret—she *loves* that snow and ice).

A unique experience for us in the South had to do with ATM machines. It seems rare that banks there have walk-up ATM machines, either inside or outside. The typical branch bank is simply not designed for use by pedestrians. And since our typical transaction involved using an ATM card to withdraw cash from an out-of-state bank, the tellers inside were unable to help us. We therefore became accustomed to standing and moving along in a line of cars to use the drive-through ATM machines, much to the amusement of the soccer moms high in their SUVs and the good ole' boys in their pickups. We, of course, were happy to entertain them, and were pleased that we could bring some pleasure into their lives.

Mail Call at Beaufort

THE INTRACOASTAL WATERWAY leaves Pamlico Sound and the Neuse River via Adams Creek and the Adams Creek Canal, and heads south to Beaufort and Morehead City on the coast. Beaufort is a single day's run from New Bern.

One of our most exciting moments in North Carolina was arriving in Beaufort at about 4:30 in the

Left, the Dockhouse Restaurant in Beaufort where we enjoyed our mail package. Right, a cruising family leaving the dinghy dock and heading out to their boat which is anchored across the channel from the Town Docks. Photos courtesy of Claiborne S. Young.

afternoon, and rushing across the before it closed. The Town Dock at Beaufort gives new arrivals coupons for free drafts of beer at their dockside restaurant, so Margaret and I sat enjoying our cold brews while we went through our latest mail bag containing new pictures of our grandson, Griffin, and other treats from Stewart and Ellen. An important aspect of the cruising life is the greatly enhanced enjoyment one gets from the simple pleasures.

Beaufort is a major stopover in the annual parade of snowbirds heading south down the Waterway, and is an extremely yachty place, with boats of all sizes and descriptions tied up and anchored just across the channel. It is also an important provisioning and jumping off place for those headed outside to the Bahamas and the Caribbean.

Our stay at Beaufort was too short to enjoy its many attractions; we thought that perhaps we would plan a longer stay on the way home. We did see wild horses grazing the sea grass on Carrot Island, across the channel and anchorage from our dock.

From the Newsletter, October 26: North Carolina Goodbye

G ETTING OUT OF the Beaufort area was difficult because the skipper misread what he was seeing. This is something that you need to constantly guard against when piloting through an unfamiliar area. You have to be ready to challenge your assumptions about what you think you are seeing. I was convinced that a high level bridge in view was a certain bridge on the chart, when in fact it was another bridge altogether. This headed us in the wrong direction into shallow water, and it took us an anxious while to sort this out and get back on track.

We then had an uneventful four-day run down the Waterway behind barrier islands, stopping at Swansboro, Hampstead, and Wrightsville Beach. The only sour note was the last leg transiting Snow's Cut (narrow, with very strong current) and motoring down the Cape Fear River to the marina on Bald Head Island. We hate the Cape Fear River. There are Waterway buoys and buoys marking the ship channel to Wilmington, and they all seemed to have been renumbered since our chart was printed. With the current against us, it was just one of those all-around unpleasant days.

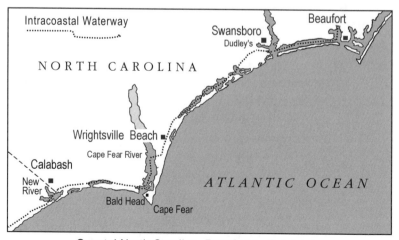

Coastal North Carolina, Beaufort to Calabash

Cape Fear itself is the outermost projection into the Atlantic of Bald Head Island. To get into the marina, you leave the Waterway and follow the main ship channel that leads out into the Atlantic.

~ ~ ~ ~ ~ ~

And so that pretty much brings us up to where we are this drizzly Sunday afternoon here on Bald Head Island. Tomorrow, weather permitting, we've got a nice 40-mile stretch down to the New River and Calabash on the South Carolina border. Glory Hallelujah! . . . . South Carolina is the Fried Seafood State, and Calabash is the fried seafood capitol of the *world!*

Margaret Speaks

MANY OF YOU PROBABLY think that Steve has muzzled me or maybe made me walk the plank. Both are true. But I nevertheless will continue to put in my own two cents—which is about all I've got, because after 40 years of my managing the money, *he's* managing the cruise budget. Heaven help us!

The weather has not been as warm as I expected this far south, but with several layers of clothing it has been tolerable. In this cruising lifestyle, you are outdoors most of the time.

While the Skipper has been doing his boat and bookkeeping, I've been doing some sightseeing. At Bath I enjoyed touring several restored houses dating back to pre-Revolutionary times, and at New Bern we both toured the restored Governor's Palace.

Just a word about this snowbird business. Yes, it is true that I like the change of seasons and don't mind those Northern winters that apparently give Steve such a problem. But one would think he could put his prejudices aside and clear the snow off the driveway once in a while!

Hmmm . . . God put it there, and God'l take it away.

The Low Country

We make it Through the Rock Pile

BETWEEN THE BEAUFORT/MOREHEAD CITY area and Calabash on the South Carolina border, the Waterway is pretty much a straight shot, running just behind the narrow barrier islands. In South Carolina and Georgia, however, it tends to run inland through rivers and land cuts and across open bays and sounds. When it does run close to the Atlantic, it crosses numerous inlets where ocean breakers and tide rips can occur close to the channel edge, causing crosscurrents and shifting shoals.

After crossing into South Carolina there is a 30-mile section called Pine Island Cut, which includes a hazardous segment known as the "Rock Pile". It is narrow, with submerged rocky ledges on both sides of the channel. There is barely room for two recreational boats to pass. There is *not* enough room to pass a barge, or to be passed by a barge, without somebody hitting the jagged rocks.

Most tug captains, and skippers of recreational boats who are aware of this hazard, call on the radio before entering this section to find out if any traffic is coming the other way. We did also—there were no big boats coming, and we got through safely. We used our "stalking horse" technique—that is, we followed <u>exactly</u> in the track of another sailboat just ahead of us that had a deeper keel than ours. Near the end of the section, *he* did hit something, but managed to get clear with no apparent damage. We were able to scoot on past after making certain that he didn't need help.

Our routine as we worked our way down through South Carolina and Georgia was to anchor two to four nights a week, spending the other nights at marinas. Our marina stays were either one-night stands or extended visits (two or more nights) at places where we planned to stop for a while. Of course, bad weather sometimes pinned us down.

Margaret schmoozing the dock at Marsh Harbor Marina, up Calabash Creek. Calabash is famous for fried seafood, and on-site gustatory research enables me to confirm that this reputation is well deserved. The boat behind her is *Gypsy* from Houston.

The Waterway was a busy place through this region, with tugs and "tows" (barges that are usually pushed and rarely towed), shrimp boats in the sounds and inlets, and many snowbirds like us headed south.

On to Georgetown

THE WACCAMAW RIVER, which the Waterway joins after the Pine Island Cut, winds lazily southward 22 miles until it intersects the headwaters of Winyah Bay near Georgetown. The Waccamaw is a magnificent stretch of the Waterway—an area of marshes, swamps, dense forests and deep creeks. Abandoned rice fields with unused

Map of coastal South Carolina showing the track of the Intracoastal Waterway.

The Georgetown shrimp fleet. Note that the tops of the masts and booms are painted white—tradition says that this is so that if the boat gets into trouble, the hand of God will have a clean place to grab to pull it out of danger.

canals, overhung by live oaks draped with Spanish moss, can be seen on both sides. Prince Creek, which branches off the Waccamaw and rejoins it about two miles down stream, is quiet, narrow, and deep. We spent a peaceful night swinging gently to our anchor in Prince Creek, with the untouched forest close on both sides and the moonlight finding us down between the overhanging trees.

Before the Civil War, Georgetown was the center of a rich rice culture, which is still remembered and celebrated locally. We stayed several days in Georgetown, tied up downtown at the friendly Boat Shed Marina, surrounded by the shrimp fleet. We did a mountain of laundry, refilled a propane tank, relished a pleasant shore dinner, and walked the nearby historic district. We particularly enjoyed visiting Prince George Episcopal Church, Winyah, with its box pews and shady graveyard with headstones dating from the early 1700's.

Halloween caught us in Georgetown, and our floating home was visited by more trick-'n-treaters than we usually get at home in Bay Village. (We live on a busy, through street.) The kids were in costume, and came from another boat tied up across the way from us. We were ready, having set up a plate of goodies on the cockpit table, illuminated by scary candles.

Margaret enjoyed a Halloween tour that included frightening stories involving several of the historic houses around town, including one within sight of our dock. I did not go, nor did the sea kitty; we have low thresholds of scare.

One of my brothers lives in Columbia, South Carolina. He and his wife picked us up in Georgetown for a drive to Charleston, where they treated us to a glorious weekend of sightseeing and eating. Charleston is a marvelous place, and we loved every minute.

This Ain't Home

WE DELIGHTED IN THE NAMES of the rivers and streams throughout this region. If you have lived in the North all of your life, you can never doubt that you are in a completely different world: Great Pee Dee River, Wapoo Creek, Ashepoo River, Dahoo River, Coosaw River, Wahoo River. The names of some of the places where we anchored between Georgetown and the Florida line tell the same colorful story: Five Fathom Creek, Oyster House Creek, Ashepoo-Coosaw Cut-Off, Turtle Island, Kilkenny Creek, New Teakettle Creek. Traveling on a small boat through this coastal world of shrimpers, fishermen, boaters and yachties

Charleston street scenes: left, St. Philip's Episcopal Church, and right, Margaret exploring with my brother, Joe Watterson.

at seven miles an hour connects you with the land and the people in a way not possible for motorists flashing through on I-95.

This brings up an interesting phenomenon dealing with physical proximity and cultural distance. There were two places on our cruise to this point where the ICW runs very close to busy highways. One was on the Dismal Swamp Canal at the North Carolina Visitors' Center. The other was the Pine Island Cut, which runs behind Myrtle Beach, just a couple of hundred feet from the billboards, traffic lights, strip malls and fast food restaurants which line Route 17. Only a narrow strip of brush and trees separates all this from the Waterway, which is slightly sunken. You are hardly aware of the highway and all its activity from the Waterway, and people on the highway have no idea that the Waterway is even there. Indeed, most of them would doubtless be surprised to learn that such a thing exists, let alone that there is a whole busy world of families who live on their boats while traveling up and down the East Coast.

By the way, if you were to ask about the difference between boaters and yachties, I would say that the dividing line lies at around $70,000 to $80,000—representing either boat price or annual income. We are boaters.

The Low Country Beckons

THE TRUE LOW COUNTRY begins south of Charleston, where deep forests give away to broad, flat marshland crisscrossed by the wide rivers and narrow creeks that wander through the great Sea Islands of southern South Carolina and Georgia. Between Charleston and Fernandina Beach on the Florida line, the world is a different and beautiful place. The Waterway winds through oceans of brilliant yellow marsh grass, tracing sinuous paths as it snakes its way among the green, wooded islands. It also runs through broad rivers and crosses wide sounds that are open to the Atlantic. The shrimp fleets ply their trade

View from the anchorage in Oyster House Creek. We tried to get in here again on the trip home, but it was badly shoaled, so we went up to New Cut Landing.

on these sounds. With net booms and outriggers extended off each side, and enveloped by canopies of fluttering scavenger gulls, the boats sweep slowly back and forth across the sparkling waters. It is amazing that there are any shrimp left.

Six to ten foot tides cause swift currents throughout this region. Channels are frequently marked by ranges. A range is a pair of markers with highly visible vertical lines on them, a low marker in front paired with a similar but higher marker a couple of hundred feet behind the low one. You stay in the channel by moving toward and watching the range markers, keeping the vertical lines on the two markers aligned—one above the other.

This is only moderately difficult when it is a front range, i.e., when you are steering towards the range markers. It is a bit more of a challenge to stay in the channel when the markers comprise a back range—when you are steering *away* from the range markers. Oh well. We chose this over ocean voyaging, so we just had to live with it.

The *Waterway Guide Chartbook, Norfolk to Jacksonville,* and the Mid-Atlantic edition of Walter's *Waterway Guide* continued to serve us well in the Low Country. In addition, the mile-by-mile format of *The Intracoastal Waterway Norfolk to Miami: a Cockpit Cruising Handbook* rendered that work indispensable.

In addition, after leaving the Erie Canal, we kept in the cockpit an ordinary road map, folded open to the area we were in. Charts are needed to navigate the waterways but they tend to have a narrow focus. Road maps are useful to tell you where you *really* are in the broader context of nearby cities and towns.

Charts, maps, and books in the cockpit were kept in zip-lock bags or in large, heavier gage zip-lock sleeves. Big, clamp-style paper clips kept the books open to the appropriate pages.

Midnight in the Garden, Etc.

THUNDERBOLT, GEORGIA is just outside of Savannah, and it is where most cruising boats visiting Savannah tie up. The Savannah River does go downtown, but the only decent dockage there is at the Hyatt Regency Hotel, which is extremely expensive. We docked at Tidewater Boat Works in Thunderbolt, a friendly, reasonably priced establishment, a mere ten-minute drive away. Kerry and Joann came down from Washington to spend the weekend with us in this wonderful city, so well captured in John Berendt's engrossing book, *Midnight in the Garden of Good and Evil.*

Savannah is absolutely unique among cities. The historic downtown is laid out in a grid pattern, with 22 lush green squares spaced at regular intervals. Under a canopy of live oaks and Spanish moss, they are like the rooms of an elegant open air mansion. But Savannah's physical attributes, while charming, cannot fully account for her allure. The extraordinary ingredient that sets Savannah apart is *attitude.* It is an intangible quality, and I wish I possessed the verbal skills to explain it to you. Spend time in Savannah, and you will feel it.

Savannah invites comparison with Charleston, another rare treasure. Of the two, I think Charleston is more attractive, architecturally more interesting, and more photogenic. But Savannah, with her worldly *panache,* wins.

Under the spell cast by *Midnight in the Garden of Good and Evil,* we checked out the Mercer house and

Savannah scenes. Mercer house, built by Johnny Mercer's great-grandfather and site of the murder portrayed in *Midnight,* at upper right. Mercer house and fountain photos courtesy of the Official Map Company.

visited the Bonaventure Cemetary, where Minerva, the voodoo priestess works her magic at midnight. The house is not open to the public, but viewing it from the square, one can easily visualize the events described in Berendt's book. One of the things that makes this book so special is that it is all true—the people are real, and it all really happened. The drag queen, The Lady Chablis, still entertains at Club One on occasional weekends.

We also enjoyed a horse-drawn carriage sightseeing tour, went through the Julliette Low house (founder of the Girl Scouts), and visited the Art Museum.

Johnny Mercer, lyricist, composer, and towering figure in American popular culture was born and raised in Savannah. If you are of my generation, he shaped your life: *Accentuate the Positive. . Jeepers Creepers. . On the Atchison, Topeka and the Santa Fe . . Goody Goody . . Lazy Bones . . Laura . . You Must Have Been a Beautiful*

*Baby . . That Old Black Magic . . Days of Wine and Roses
. . In the Cool, Cool, Cool of the Evening . . Moon River.*

There is no direct connection between Johnny Mercer and the events portrayed in *Midnight in the Garden of Good and Evil* (the Mercer house is no longer owned by the Mercer family). But his story is so intertwined with the city that for me he an integral part of the Savannah mystique that permeates Berendt's book.

Johnny Mercer is buried in the Bonaventure Cemetery with his wife. The inscription on Ginger Mercer's tombstone reads, *"You must have been a beautiful baby."* His reads, *". . . and the angels sing".* The cemetery overlooks the Waterway (right next to where we were docked), and one of the branching creeks downstream just south of town is named *"Moon River".*

Savannah is simply enchanting.

From the Newsletter, December 5: A Georgia Day on the Waterway

6:45 AM   I get up . . . it seems cold . . . I turn off the anchor light, slide open the companionway hatch and stick my head out to check Kilkenny Creek, where we are anchored. One boat has already left the anchorage, leaving four including us. The sun has just cleared the horizon . . . there are no clouds . . . it's going to be a wonderful day. The world is endless yellow marsh grass punctuated by dark green islands of live oak, cabbage palmetto, and pine . . . the sky is turning clear blue . . . it is beautiful. The current has reversed . . . we are facing in the opposite direction from when we anchored yesterday afternoon. I turn on the instruments and note that the water depth is now 13 feet vs. 18 feet yesterday . . . the tide is going out . . . I note that the speed of the current is 1.4 knots. A file of pelicans glides down and silently skims the surface of the creek next to the boat, outstretched wings motionless . . .

they swoop up and are gone. I go below, light the propane heater and turn on the TV for news and weather. Margaret is up, fixing breakfast . . . cold cereal, bananas, milk, buttered toast with marmalade, coffee and tea.

Map of Coastal Georgia

7:30 AM Breakfast is finished and put away . . . propane and TV turned off. We review the day's run . . . Margaret circles key aids to navigation and makes notes in the chartbook and the Moellers' cockpit handbook. If we were in the open waters of the Chesapeake or in Albemarle or Pamlico Sounds, I would be entering waypoints on the GPS, but here in Georgia we'll be in rivers and land cuts most of the day . . . we will be crossing St. Catherine's and Sapelo Sounds, but the distances suggest that we ought to be able to spot the navigation aids with binoculars . . . . . the Moellers' handbook gives compass courses in case the visibility gets bad. Our destination today is the Golden Isles Marina on St. Simon's Island where we made a reservation by cell phone . . . we plan dinner with Miata Club friends at St. Simon's. . . we hope they will have a mail parcel for us from Stewart and Ellen. The day's run will be 65 statute miles, or 56.5 nautical miles . . . at six knots (nautical miles per hour) it will take us about nine and a half hours . . our ETA is about 5:30PM . . . this will be an unusually long run for us . . . on a typical day we travel 30 to 45 nautical miles.

7:45 AM We prepare for departure . . . Margaret secures below and I check oil, belts, hoses, and start the engine. I prepare the cockpit by bringing up binoculars, hand-held VHF radio, air horn, chart book, waterway handbook, map, gloves, sun glasses, reading glasses, and portable radio for Dr. Laura and tunes. Each item is stowed in its accustomed place for quick retrieval . . . I buckle my watch to the pedestal stanchion for easy viewing . . . the engine is idling, warming. I wave to another departing snowbird and go below to suit up . . . it is 43 °F, will go to 68° . . . I layer sweatshirts and nylon shell for peeling as it warms up.

7:55 AM We are both on deck . . . Margaret is at the bow, pulling the boat up to the anchor . . . when the boat is over the anchor, she cleats the anchor line and signals ready. Our "Max" anchor buries itself so well that it invariably needs to be powered out. I power ahead . . . 1.5 knots . . . 1.8 knots . . . . the bow dips down, comes up . . . the anchor is free. I slow the boat . . . Margaret gets the anchor up, and as she is stowing it on the bow roller, I motor slowly out of the anchorage . . . there is one boat left . . . the catamaran from New Jersey . . . we wave as we go by. I head down the Waterway.

9:00 AM We are entering St. Catherine's Sound and heading for the entrance to the North Newport River . . . this is a fairly straight stretch . . . the wind is on our beam and we are motorsailing with the jib unfurled. This increases our speed by about one knot, and makes us feel more like a sailboat. The knot meter reads 7.4 to 7.6, but I know we are running against a current, which increases the speed of the water past the hull . . . Margaret goes below to check our SOGs (Speed Over the Ground) on the GPS . . . she reports that we are actually moving across the earth's surface at 5.2 knots. I wonder what sane person would travel from Cleveland to Key West at the speed of a fast walk . . . but when we motorsail *with* the current, we get SOGs in the mid-to-high 8's, which makes us feel good. Margaret is spotting the Waterway markers for me with the binoculars . . . they are red triangles and green squares, and they indicate the location of the channel . . . the water can get very shallow outside the channel, and running aground is a constant concern. It can be difficult to distinguish between the Waterway markers and the markers and buoys placed to guide boats traveling up the sound from the Atlantic . . . confusion here can result in a grounding. We pass a slower sailboat, and are passed in turn by several large powerboats. Shrimp boats are at work, sweeping the sound . . . they move slowly . . . with their outriggers and net booms extended they look in the distance like French nun's caps . . . Margaret says St. Vincent de Paul.

Shrimper sweeping St. Catherine's
Sound

12:00 NOON Margaret has the helm and I have
been spotting markers for her, checking them on the chart.
The jib is furled . . . . we have been winding through an
endless sea of yellow marsh grass for a couple of hours . .
we see a pair of Bald Eagles high in a tree as we skirt a
dense green island. The route is so circuitous that in the
distance off to the side, we see other sailboats which seem
to be headed back from where we came from, but which
are actually ahead of us traveling down the Waterway . .
they look as if they are sailing on a flat ocean of sun-
sparkled grass. I go below to get lunch . . . Diet Coke
(Margaret), V-8 juice (Steve), cheese, crackers, cookies,
apples. On cool, cloudy days I might fix steaming mugs of
soup . . . but today, this will be just fine.

4:30 PM The sun is warm, the sky is blue, and
all is well . . we have shed sweatshirts and sweaters, and
are snacking on grapes, cookies and Coke. We are in a
section of winding rivers with connecting land cuts . . .
there are numerous front and back ranges to be followed.
Pukka the sea kitty graced the cockpit with her presence
for a while, staring intently at the passing water, but soon
got bored and went below to curl up in her spot on the
berth in the forward cabin . . . she missed out on a file of
pelicans and some porpoises, which would have gotten
her serious attention. We see what appears to be a huge
cruise ship coming up behind us . . . turns out to be the
Nantucket Clipper . . . not huge, but at 100 passengers big
for these waters. We had chatted with her crew a couple of
weeks ago when we were both tied up at Beaufort, South

Carolina . . . she was embarking passengers for a golf cruise . . . we know of her because she occasionally cruises the Great Lakes in the summer. We slow down so that we will be in a wide stretch when she passes . . . she draws eight feet, and we wonder how she gets through the places where our depth sounder indicates five or six feet . . . to say nothing about the places where we touch the mud . . . I guess her skipper knows where the deep water is . . . I wish I did.

6:30 PM We are docked along side at Golden Isles on St. Simon's, which turns out to be an exceptionally fine marina. Fuel and water are topped off . . . the deck hosed down . . . we are showered and dressed for dinner . . . Chris and Connie will be picking us up soon. The boat tied up in front of us is *Magnolia,* an immaculate trawler . . . I call them the clean boat people, and wonder how their boat stays so clean. I find out over the next couple of weeks as we meet at various ports of call . . . they are both constantly washing their boat. The boat docked behind us is *Surrender,* a Hunter 34 from Bay Point Marina, across the Bay from our home dock in Sandusky. We enjoy a delightful dinner with our friends, and retire back on the boat to check out the mail package and rest for an exciting day tomorrow . . . tomorrow night we will be in *Florida!*

There is just something inherently photogenic about shrimpers

6

Down the Sunshine Coast

Warm at Last!

FERNANDINA BEACH, FLORIDA, is one day's run south of St. Simon's Island. Boaters cross the state line at red buoy 32, which is practically in sight of the Fernandina Beach harbor. As we passed the buoy, it *instantly* got warmer— Margaret and I scrambled for sun block and shades, while Pukka went tearing through her stuff screaming, "*who took my bikini!!?*" As we neared the harbor we were overtaken by *Early Out*, a Tartan 40 that crossed the Erie Canal with us, but which we had not seen since the upper Hudson. Also with us at Fernandina Beach were *Agrippina* from Ottawa, with whom we shared the Kilkenny Creek anchorage, and of course the clean boat people busily washing *Magnolia*.

Our disappointment on learning that the Florida Welcome Center had been closed down (no welcoming glass of golden juice!) was ameliorated somewhat by a delightful pub grub dinner at O'Kane's Irish Grille, located on the pretty main street and an easy walk from the water. Fernandina Beach is an historic and attractive place, with many nearby restaurants to chose from. We decided to keep on truckin', so we did not stay longer than one night; we made a note to spend a few days there on the way home in the spring.

Working our way on down Florida's East Coast, we alternated between spending nights at anchor and tying up at marinas. The Waterway tends to be straighter here than it was in Georgia, although there are some wandering sections, and piloting across the open ocean inlets and rivers keeps you on your toes. The long straight sections are ideal for motorsailing, except south of the Palm Beaches where there are too many bridges to be fooling around with the sails. We saw another bald eagle, and the porpoises and pelicans continued to entertain us. We spotted an alligator hungrily eyeing our kitty.

There is a suburb of Cleveland known for pink plastic flamingos on front lawns. It is not far from where we live. We felt right at home in one section of northern Florida, where many of the lawns sloping down to the Waterway are decorated with plastic pelicans.

St. Augustine

THE AFTERNOON AND EVENING we spent walking St. Augustine were delightful. The very old part of the city is unfortunately highly commercialized—houses and other buildings dating from the earliest Spanish settlement in the late 1500's are now souvenir shops. These are the oldest structures in the hemisphere built by Europeans (I think this is so, but I'm prepared to be corrected), so it's something of a surprise to find yourself in one of these buildings elbowing your way through a crowd of people checking out the T-shirt and trinket displays and buying ice cream. Perhaps the buildings on these narrow streets are reconstructions. In any event, once you get over the shock, it is fun.

St. Augustine: cruising boats anchored off Castillo de San Marcos, left. Right, a classic cruiser motors through the Bridge of Lions. Both of these photos were taken from our cockpit while anchored just several hundred feet off downtown.

But we enjoyed walking through the restored *old* sections of the city (1700's and early 1800's) more than our tour of the *very old* section (1500's and 1600's), which is the commercialized tourist district.

Most interesting for me, however, were the monumental buildings built in the 1880's and 1890's by Henry Flagler in a romantic Spanish/Moorish/Romanesque style. The red tile roofs of a large hotel (now Flagler College), a magnificent church, and city and county administration complexes designed in this style dominate the center of St. Augustine. One of the interesting features of the Flagler buildings is that they were built of poured concrete, with inlaid brick and terra cotta trim, the exterior surfaces clearly showing the textures and patterns of the wooden forms.

This Man Was a Visionary

H ENRY FLAGLER DESERVES a brief mention here because he had so much to do with the development of Florida's East Coast. Like me, Henry was an Ohioan born in New York, but unlike me, he was an early partner of John D. Rockefeller in Standard Oil (damn! missed it again). In 1883 he traveled to St. Augustine with his wife and liked it a lot, but found the hotel and transportation facilities to be inadequate. Recognizing Florida's potential for attracting visitors from the North, Henry withdrew

Built by Henry Flagler as the Hotel Ponce de Leon in 1888, this building is now a part of Flagler College. Eclectic and wildly romantic in style, it pioneered poured concrete construction.

from his day-to-day involvement with Standard Oil (he remained on the Board of Directors) in order to pursue his interests in Florida.

In 1885, he began construction of the 540-room Hotel Ponce de Leon in St. Augustine. It opened in 1888 and was an instant success. Meanwhile, he had bought the Jacksonville, St. Augustine and Halifax Railroad, and after the hotel opened, he built a railroad bridge across the St. Johns River to gain tourist access to the southern part of the state. Henry understood the need for a good transportation system to support his hotel ventures.

In 1890, Henry bought the Ormond Beach Hotel just north of Daytona, and shortly afterwards began construction of his own home, Kirkside, in St. Augustine.

In 1894, he completed the Royal Poinciana Hotel on the shores of Lake Worth in Palm Beach. The world's largest wooden structure, the Royal Poinciana was designed to accommodate 1500 guests—more than the population of Palm Beach at the time. As Henry pushed his rail line south from Jacksonville to West Palm Beach, resort towns sprang up in its wake. With his railroad (by now renamed The Florida East Coast Railway), this man single-handedly created a boom in tourism and development the likes of which had never been seen anywhere. Two years later, Henry built the Palm Beach Inn (later re-named The Breakers) overlooking the Atlantic.

Henry had originally intended West Palm Beach to be the terminus of his railroad system, but he was pressured by two owners of large tracts of land in the southern part of the state, Julia Tuttle and William Brickell, to extend the railroad south to Biscayne Bay.

The issue was resolved in the winter of 1894-1895. Severe freezes hit central Florida, costing Henry thousands of dollars in lost revenue because the citrus growers had no fruit to ship on his railroad. Julia sent Henry an orange blossom to remind him that it doesn't freeze in Miami. This plus other sweeteners, like land, convinced Henry to bring his rail line on down. It reached Biscayne Bay in 1896, and Miami's boom was born. Henry dredged channels, built streets, instituted the first water and power systems, financed the town's first newspaper, and built the Royal Palm Hotel.

At this time, Key West was Florida's most populous city, and the United States' closest deep-water port to the canal that the U.S. government was proposing to build in what is now Panama. Already a bustling commercial center, it was poised to benefit from the increased trade with Cuba, Latin America, and the West that the new canal would bring.

In 1905, Henry Flagler fulfilled his destiny by pushing his railroad on down to the southwest, bridging

Henry Flagler built this church in St. Augustine. It is a feast for the eyes.

the hundreds of islands that make up the Florida Keys. On January 22, 1912, he rode the first train from Miami to Key West, traveling the 130 miles in his private rail car, *Rambler*. The Key West Extension had cost many millions of his dollars and required thousands of workers. Water, food, clothing, shelter, tools, and building materials—all had to be supplied by barges.

When he arrived in Key West that day, Henry Flagler was applauded by more than 10,000 spectators and dignitaries. His railroad could go no further. The following year, his work done, Henry Flagler passed away. He rests in St. Augustine, alongside his daughter, Jennie Louise, and his first wife, Mary Harkness.

~   ~   ~   ~   ~   ~

We were in St. Augustine on the night that the Christmas decorations were lighted downtown in the wonderful outdoor spaces on the riverfront, near the Castillo de San Marcos (Spanish fort, 1695) and the Bridge of Lions. The decorations consisted of lights strung through the canopy of trees that graces this district, and on the balustrade that runs along the river's edge. It was very pretty.

I know . . . I know. Christmas lights are Christmas lights . . . we have all seen Christmas lights . . . why are we describing Christmas lights? Well, as I have noted, when you are cruising far from home, you tend to focus on simple things and take pleasure from ordinary sights and events that in a home environment would be unremarkable. Besides, these were not the Bay Village, Ohio Christmas lights . . . we're talkin' *St. Augustine* here!

We Spot the VAB

THE KENNEDY SPACE CENTER is on Merritt Island, across the Indian River from Titusville. It is surrounded by the Merritt Island National Wildlife Refuge and dominated by the colossal Vehicle Assembly Building, which becomes

The Vehicle Assembly Building at the Kennedy Space Center. Photo courtesy of NASA.

visible to approaching boaters nearly 20 miles away. Spotting the VAB was exciting for me, because it meant we were getting close to the Titusville/Cocoa area where my parents lived after my Dad retired.

We spent several days (including Thanksgiving) at the Titusville Municipal Marina, and we could not have picked a more congenial place. It was like old home week—*Surrender* from Bay Point, Ohio, *Gypsy,* a baby schooner from Houston we last saw in Calabash, North Carolina, *Early Out, Aggrippina, Magnolia* getting a bath, and others—each with a story to tell.

On Thanksgiving Day we walked a couple of miles to volunteer at the Salvation Army. We washed pots while hundreds of meals were served (we did manage to sneak a few pieces of turkey). Later in the day, back at the marina, cruising families got together a potluck Thanksgiving dinner under one of the pavilions. Along with 30 or so other people, we stuffed ourselves with more turkey and all kinds of other treats. All this with porpoises and manatees frolicking in the marina fairways—what a blast!

The day after Thanksgiving we rented a car and drove to West Marine (a boating supply store) in Melbourne to pick up a new anchor line. We had wrapped an anchor line around the prop shaft while anchoring in Daytona Beach; a diver freed it, but it was badly chewed up. We were lucky not to have lost the anchor.

(No fun being reminded of *that* experience—it was white-knuckle time again as I unwisely tried to maneuver while anchoring, and somehow over-rode the line. A call to the Boat/US 800 number on the cell phone set up a 3-way call between Boat/US, a local tow firm, and us. They had a diver on staff, and he was there in 20 minutes. Talk about feeling stupid! And, to make matters worse, since I needed a diver and not a tow, the incident was not covered by the insurance that comes with Boat/US membership.)

After West Marine, we checked out several family venues in the area, with both happy and happy/sad associations for us, and then drove to the beautiful cemetary in Mt. Dora where my father and stepmother rest. Mt. Dora is a charming lake country town in the central part of the state.

That evening, we were treated to an informal Country and Western concert at the marina. I'm not a Country and Western fan, but this was a delight because it

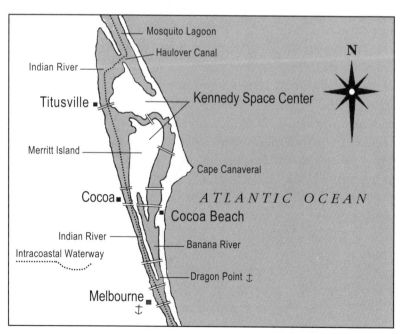

Florida's Space Coast, showing the track of the Intracoastal Waterway.

was live and because these musicians were good. They are retired professional performers who live in the area. They get together on Friday nights to put on a show for the cruising families.

Bridge, Anyone?

CONTINUING ON SOUTH, we spent nights at anchor in Cocoa, Jensen Beach, and Palm Beach. At Palm Beach we anchored in Lake Worth near Peanut Island, just south of the Lake Worth Inlet, and at Jensen Beach we anchored in the lee of the causeway leading to the Jensen Beach Bridge; bad weather pinned us down there for two nights. We stayed at marinas at Vero Beach and at Delray Beach.

This is a stretch of the Waterway with a lot of bridges. Between Titusville and the Las Olas Boulevard Bridge in Fort Lauderdale, there are 31 bridges that have to open for cruising sailboats; 30 of these are in the 99 miles between Fort Pierce and Fort Lauderdale. Although some of these open on request, most open only on their own schedule. Of course, each bridge's schedule is different. Here's the opening schedule for the PGA Boulevard Bridge in North Palm Beach. It is typical:

Year Round Mon-Fri	7am to 9am, 4pm to 7pm opens at :15 and :45 past the hour
Wknd & Hldy	8am to 6pm opens on the hour and every :20 thereafter
Nov 1 to Apr 30 Mon- Fri	9am to 4pm opens on the hour and every :20 thereafter

What this bridge does between 9am and 4pm year round and after 4pm in the summer is not clear. Actually, it opens on demand. But, you wind up talking with the bridge tender. Many bridges simply don't open for 2 hours during morning and afternoon rush hours. So the bridges rule your schedule, and you learn to relax and go with the flow. You are either pokin' along because the next one won't be opening for another hour, or you are racing to make the next one because if you miss it you are going to be circling for 30 minutes.

Between the Palm Beaches and Fort Lauderdale, the Waterway loses its semi-wild character and becomes a busy marine highway running through *very* affluent neighborhoods. And between Lauderdale and Miami it is a concrete trench running in a canyon formed by high-rise condominiums.

Fort Lauderdale

FOR BOATING PEOPLE, Fort Lauderdale is an amazing place. Thousands of boats of all sizes and descriptions tied up at marinas and along the hundreds of miles of house-lined canals provide a visual feast. Approaching the city from the north via the Waterway is an incredible experience because of the proliferation of mega-yachts tied up one after another—150 to 200 foot yachts, each one worth many millions.

Fort Lauderdale does an excellent job accommodating boaters. With its endless variety of marinas and boatyards offering every conceivable marine service to yachtsmen, it truly is the "Yachting Capital of the World", and the municipal facilities for transient boaters are outstanding. We stayed at the municipal docks at Cooley's Landing on the New River, which branches off the Intracoastal and winds through the heart of the city.

Riverwalk Park borders the New River adjacent to Cooley's Landing. Many services are available to boats tied up along the River, including a roving fuel barge, and the Turd Tug. Photo courtesy of Claiborne S. Young.

Left, the dock at Cooley's Landing with the Third Avenue Bridge in the background. Right, the laundry and facilities at Cooley's are top notch.

Going up the New River for the first time was a harrowing experience, scoring about 2.5 on the anxiety scale. It is narrow, winding, lined with tied-up boats of all sizes, full of traffic in both directions, and crossed by bridges which will open if you ask (but you gotta ask nice, and they can't always open just then because of heavy car traffic). There is a fair current in the river, and there is little room to circle while waiting for the bridge to open, because there are too many other boats with the same problem. The *Jungle Queen,* a large tourist excursion boat plies the river; on the water, as in most of life, the 800-lb. gorilla has the right of way. When that thing is coming at you in a very narrow place where there's no room to pass (and he couldn't stop if he tried), you do wonder why you enjoy this so much. All this marvelous activity is fun to watch from shore and hell to watch from mid-channel.

Cooley's Landing is located in the wonderfully landscaped Riverwalk Park, which stretches along the river's northerly bank. With coconut palms and brilliantly blooming red hibiscus set in well-tended, landscaped grounds, it is a delightful place to spend a few days. The extensive laundry and other facilities are new and air-conditioned. It was also relatively inexpensive.

We stayed for a week, relishing the continual procession of boats of all sizes up and down the river. One night there was a Christmas "Parade of Lights" out on the Intracoastal. We enjoyed watching the extravagantly lit

The delightful Lauderdale December weather did not dampen our Christmas spirit. Left, *Witch of Endor* sports a mast wreath; above, our Christmas tree on the saloon table.

and decorated boats, loaded with loud music and partying people, going down river to join the festivities. Later that night, in the pouring rain, we also enjoyed watching the same folks returning—subdued, soaked, and sober.

We spent the lazy, sunny afternoons at Cooley's Landing putting up our little Christmas tree and decorating the boat while playing Christmas tapes. We also plotted GPS waypoints for the four-day run to our Christmas destination—Boot Key Harbor at Marathon in the Keys. In addition, we enjoyed a pleasant visit by the son of dockmates of ours in Sandusky. He is a US Coast Guard-licensed delivery captain with numerous trips through the keys under his belt, and he gave us many useful pointers on routes and anchorages.

Several major cultural attractions are located along the Riverwalk Park, including the Center for Performing Arts, the Art Museum, and the Science Museum. We walked the Riverwalk to shops and the supermarket, and took the bus to a large mall for Christmas shopping.

One of the other boats at Cooley's Landing was *Woodfield II*, a Nauticat 43 from the UK, which we last saw in the Chesapeake at the small marina up Indian Creek near Kilmarnock, Virginia, where we were weather-bound for several days. Later, we found this boat anchored near us in Boot Key Harbor.

A local boat yard installed a new heating element in the *Witch of Endor's* hot water heater (second time this trip). We were pleasantly surprised to find that the mechanic's hourly rate was less than what we are accustomed to in Ohio, and unlike our home marina, we were only charged for the time spent actually working on our boat, and for the materials actually used.

The Keys Beckon

B ISCAYNE BAY IS DESCRIBED in travel brochures as a "subtropical lagoon", which amused us as we bundled up in heavy jackets against the cold wind during our sail to Crandon Park Marina on Key Biscayne. High winds kept us at Crandon Park a day longer than planned, but we had a pleasant walk on a semi-wild tropical nature trail and explored the beach on the Atlantic side.

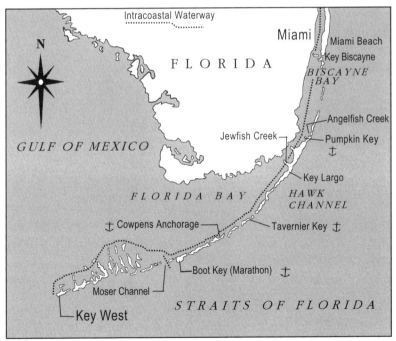

Lower Florida and the Keys. After a night at anchor at Pumpkin Key, we crossed to the Atlantic side through Angelfish Creek and enjoyed two days of sailing to Boot Key, spending the night behind Tavernier Key.

A day following the Intracoastal south through Biscayne Bay and Card Sound brought us to our planned anchorage at Pumpkin Key, a popular spot for spending the night on the Bay side of the Keys. By nightfall, there were seven boats anchored in the lee of this little island, including the catamaran *Pop Pop's Toy* from Maryland (later with us in Boot Key Harbor). Pumpkin Key reminded us of Ballast Island, which is a small island near Put-in-Bay in our Lake Erie cruising area. The residential compound and dock on shore were decorated with an illuminated Santa and Christmas lights, adding a festive note to the evening.

The next day we carefully crossed through Angelfish Ceek to the Atlantic side of the Keys. We crossed at high tide—not enough water at low tide, and barely enough at high tide—and sailed and motorsailed for two days to Boot Key harbor at Marathon, spending the night tucked in behind Tavernier Key. The Atlantic side is called Hawk Channel. It is well marked and protected from the Atlantic swell by coral reefs. The wind was 15-20 knots from the east-northeast, which put it off our quarter, and with 4-6 foot seas, we had a rollicking ride.

Our first night in Boot Key Harbor was spent tied up to the Tiki dock at Sombrero Marina and Dockside Lounge, where we were entertained well into the evening by the Florida Straits' Sunday night jam session. Boot Key is *some* place—we'll leave it for the next chapter.

From the Newsletter, December 21: Miscellany

INTERESTING FACT: The deepest water we have experienced since leaving Sandusky was in the Hudson River, where the depth sounder went to 160 feet near the Bear Mountain Bridge.

FOOD: The food on board again deserves special mention. Margaret continues to astound with her culinary feats. *Item:* Country Fried Chicken, Mashed Potatoes with Gravy, Peas, and Corn. *Item:* Pepper-Marinated Pork Loin, Noodles with

Sour Cream, and Salad. *Item:* FRESH BAKED BREAD! Yes, you read it right. When we're docked and plugged into shore power, the wonderful aroma of baking bread permeates the boat. *This is better than home!*

PUKKA: After these several months, Pukka the sea kitty, (now sporting her new Florida moniker: "'Gator Bait"), is completely acclimated to her nautical environment and the cruising way of life. At least, that is what she tells me. She's doing good with the flies, and promises to try to learn other useful boating skills.

Margaret Speaks

THE SOUTHERN ADVENTURE continues, but I'm beginning to miss the northern winter *(What did I tell you?)*, although it is cooler than normal down here because of the *el niño* effect. We're looking forward to next month— all our kids (with grandchildren) are coming down to spend a week with us. They have booked a condo at the Faro Blanco Resort in Marathon, and we have booked a dock there for the week. Can't wait!

Here's a cruising tid-bit: many women on boats bake bread. One woman on a large trawler even has a bread maker. Another Canadian/German lady has bread flour mix sent from Germany. I bake my bread on a rack in the electric fry pan, but we do need to be plugged into shore power to use the fry pan.

This is *my* bag. Stay outta *my* bag!

7

Turnaround

Christmas in the Keys

BOOT KEY HARBOR, about two-thirds of the way out the Keys at Marathon, is a well-protected anchorage that is very popular with cruisers and live-aboards. It is about one mile long and less than a half mile wide, and at any given moment is home to 80 to 120 anchored boats. It is ringed with condos, houses, and marinas set among the palms and mangrove thickets.

During the two months that we lived at anchor there, our shore base was the Sombrero Dockside Lounge. For a small weekly fee, this establishment provides a dinghy dock, bike and car parking, garbage disposal, mail address, phone messaging, book exchange, and access to ice, phones, washers and dryers, and showers. Dockside is also a bar, with food and a pleasant, covered outdoor lounge dock with nightly entertainment. It is *the* place to be in Boot Key Harbor. We spent our first night there tied

Pukka guarding the Christmas goodies, left. Right, part of the outdoor lounge at Dockside, and *Witch of Endor* at anchor in Boot Key Harbor.

up at the dockside lounge while a large crowd partied to the live music of the Florida Straits. (Fortunately, they knock off at 9 PM).

There are dinghy docks around Boot Key Harbor and you go everywhere in your dinghy. There is even a West Marine dinghy dock. If you don't feel like going someplace in your dinghy, the watertaxi will come and get you. If you need water, you call the Iceman on the radio and he'll deliver water (and pizza, but not ice). While we were there, Pastor Mike Kole held well-attended Sunday services aboard the church boat, *Isla de Ibiza,* a 110-foot schooner with awnings rigged over its spacious deck.

Outside of our floating home, Dockside was the focal point of our life at Boot Key, with its open-air snack bar and lots of room to sit around, socialize, and just hang out. Hardly a day went by without a dinghy run to Dockside, be it for shopping, to check the mail and phone board, to get some ice, to empty trash, or to make a phone call.

Shopping was easy. We took our dinghy to Dockside—a supermarket, drugstores, a K-Mart, the Post Office, the Panda House restaurant (*you guessed it*) and anything else you might need was a 10-minute walk away. We used our backpacks for shopping trips. After a few weeks, we learned how to get even closer to the stores with the dinghy, by going up one of the canals and tying up to the mangroves behind the Post Office.

On Christmas Day we enjoyed a potluck dinner at Dockside, with turkey, dressing, and gravy provided by the management, and tons of other dishes brought by the cruisers and live-aboards. We also joined the New Year's Eve party there. Thanks to Stewart and Ellen, we received a huge package of Christmas cards and gifts soon after New Year.

Picture this: It was 5 PM on January 2nd and we were lounging in our cockpit. The late afternoon sun painted shore buildings, trees, and anchored boats with liquid gold. A bright blue Florida sky arched over the shimmering blue-green water; Christmas music floated on the air and the warm breeze swayed the tops of the shoreside coconut palms. We sipped cold beer, opening family presents, and enjoying cards and notes from family and friends new and old. Surely . . . . *this* was Paradise.

Life on the Hook

L IVING AT ANCHOR for an extended period <u>does</u> have a downside, however. We had several windy spells—too windy to venture out in the dinghy without getting very

The sunsets at Boot Key Harbor range from beautiful to absolutely spectacular.

The marina at the Faro Blanco Resort on the Florida Bay side of the Keys.

wet. (Our dinghy is small). You need a lot of reading material on board, and, although I was never bored, boredom is possible.

Taking the laundry ashore could be a drag. The laundry facilities at Dockside are not extensive, and Margaret often had to wait to use the machines. I would be working on some project around the boat with the VHF radio on and tuned to channel 68 and I would hear, *"Witch of Endor, Witch of Endor,* calling *Witch of Endor".* I would reply, "This is *Witch of Endor,* go ahead." *"Witch of Endor,* this is Washerwoman. I'm going to be at least another hour here." "OK Washerwoman", I would say, "Call me when you're done."

But Margaret didn't mind terribly much, because it was a chance to hang around Dockside and get all the gossip.

In the middle of January we got the hooks up to sail over to the Faro Blanco Marina Resort, where our kids had booked a condo for a week. Faro Blanco is nearby in Marathon, but it is on the Florida Bay side of the Keys, and

Boot Key Harbor is on the ocean side. There are only a few places in the Keys where the water is deep enough to go from one side to the other in a sailboat—fortunately, one of them, the Moser Channel which goes under the Seven Mile Bridge, was not far away.

We had a wonderful week with our children and grand children, going to the beach and doing all kinds of tourist things. Margaret is going to want to tell you about this in *Margaret Speaks,* so I won't steal her thunder.

Dockside Days

AFTER THE CHILDREN LEFT, we returned to Boot Key Harbor and enjoyed the easy life of the Conch Republic for five more weeks.

Our days were filled with a variety of activities. We packed lunch and took the dinghy out Sister Creek through the mangrove islands to a wonderful protected white sand beach on the ocean side, and swam in the warm water which lays out there in all shades of green and blue. We wondered what it would be like to live on one of the little islands with houses nestled among the palms.

I worked on the diesel engine, doing maintenance and repair, changing oil and filters, and replacing the water pump and some belts and hoses. I refueled the boat from deck cans and took the dinghy to a fuel dock to get the cans filled with diesel fuel for the boat and gas for the outboard. The diesel was run for a hour or so in the morning and again around supper time to keep the batteries charged for refrigeration, lights and radios—going for fuel was a fortnightly task.

We dinghied to West Marine, Ace Hardware, and the inflatable store to get parts and supplies. We listened to Patrick (a retired musician) playing his trumpet in his cockpit. We hung around Dockside, socializing, checking mail, getting ice, doing laundry . . . (I wrote this

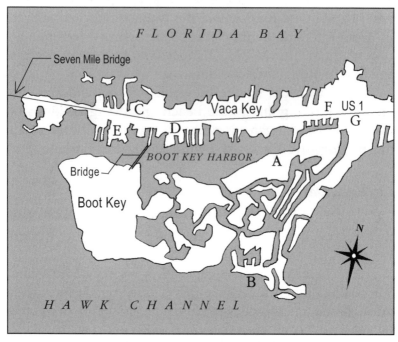

BOOT KEY HARBOR

A Dockside
B Sombrero Beach
C Faro Blanco Bayside
D West Marine, Ace Hardware

E Fuel Dock
F Post Office, Stores
G Supermarket, K-Mart, Drug Store

section perched on a stool, gazing out over the harbor, the laptop on the bar).

With two anchors set, the lines would get twisted as the wind clocked around, so from time to time it was necessary to unwind the anchor lines. This could be accomplished by pushing the boat around with the dinghy nosed against the side at the stern (if there was room amongst the other boats). Alternatively, one could deal with it at the bow by passing the entire bundle of undeployed line of one anchor many times around the other line. Either way, this chore was a first class you know what.

Clockwise from top left: *Isla de Ibiza* (the Church boat) in the distance, Sombrero Beach, and the open-air bar at Dockside.

We careened the dinghy (hauled it out and flipped it over) at the beach, scraping four months' accumulation of growth and barnacles from its bottom. (The last time we had done this was on the dock at Thunderbolt, Georgia.)

We attended Sunday services on the church boat, and had our Sunday dinners on shore at Panda House (all you could eat for $4.95—but strangely, we seemed to get hungry again in about an hour).

Witch of Endor's water tanks hold about 60 gallons, and we needed a refill every ten to twelve days. A call on the radio brought Bob the Iceman to fill the tanks. He publishes a monthly newsletter on Keys and Boot Key Harbor doings, and was a good source of info and gossip.

We lazed around the cockpit watching the world go by, reading, knitting, listening to the radio and tapes, and enjoying the sunsets, always pretty and sometimes spectacular. We made plans at Marathon Boat Yard to haul the boat out of the water in order to check out the shaft, propeller, and bottom before starting our trek back up Florida's East Coast.

The Passing Parade

OUR BOAT WAS ANCHORED near the channel, and the view from our cockpit was entertaining . . . the Conch Water Taxi making it's rounds ("Boats, Beaches, Bars, Bistros") . . . the Iceman delivering water in *Aquarius* . . . dinghies with dogs perched in the bow (always in the bow—just like dogs and car windows) . . . dinghies with little kids . . . dinghies with big kids . . . dinghies driven by kids (the number of children on cruising boats is amazing) . . . people visiting other boats, or just stopping to socialize, dinghy to cockpit . . . occasional visits to the harbor by the jackbooted Florida Marine Patrol, their boat gray and black and menacing . . . pelicans (the most stately and dignified of birds) soaring and skimming the water's surface . . . boats of many nationalities arriving and leaving . . . many Canadians, but also boats flying the ensigns of France, Italy, Belgium, England, Ireland . . . this is a busy international stopover.

A young Italian couple was anchored next to us. She was attractive, and she wore a string bikini just about all the time. It was interesting how passing dinghies seemed to slow when she was on deck—this boat was apparently on the route to every destination around the harbor. But most remarkable was that there seemed to be a kind of "Bermuda Triangle" phenomenon going on. An awful lot of outboard motors developed some sort of trouble near this boat, necessitating much stopping and tinkering. We were anchored right next door for several

Witch of Endor dozing in the sun.

Key West: street scene, left. Right, the Ernest Hemingway house. Hemingway house photo courtesy of Claiborne. S. Young.

weeks, and I was never able to figure this out. My outboard ran just fine!

Boot Key Weather

D URING OUR STAY in Boot Key Harbor, the weather ranged from perfect to awful. One day there was a very severe storm with violent wind, big waves, and thick, driving rain. We knew it was coming, and prepared for it by stowing the awning and taking the bimini down. When it began to blow hard, I started the engine and had it idling in neutral in case we needed it in a hurry.

We did. The storm caused our anchors to drag, and the minute we realized they were not holding, we donned our foul weather gear and lifejacket/harnesses and went on deck. I am always surprised at how insulated from the weather you are when below deck. I knew we were rolling and pitching and that it was raining and windy out there, but nothing prepared us for the totally uncontrolled mayhem that hit us when we stuck our heads out the companionway hatch. The boat was pitching and rolling wildly, with the wind screaming and gusts laying us over 30 to 40 degrees. The wind-driven rain cut visibility and made it difficult to see and to breathe.

The situation was lousy. Other violently bouncing boats, some of them also dragging their anchors, surrounded us. We had to get control of our boat and get the anchors on deck. I took the helm and Margaret crawled forward to the bow. We could barely see each other, let alone hear each other. I had to get underway and steer to avoid other boats, and it was essential to keep our propeller shaft and propeller away from our own and everyone else's anchor lines. If a line got wrapped around the propeller shaft, the engine would stall, and without the engine we would be helpless. I don't want to make this sound worse than it was, but it was bad. Margaret was having a wild ride couched at the bow holding on for dear life as she worked to get the anchors in. The bow was pitching up in the air 6 to 7 feet, and then plunging down, only to fly up again while the boat rolled 40 degrees in the gusts.

She managed to get both anchors on board, and somehow I kept the boat moving and under control, avoiding what I had to avoid. We were able to get over to some pilings in front of the condos, and after much effort we were securely tied and fendered.

This was a high anxiety experience. Paradise is not free, and we paid our dues that day. But we were lucky, because this storm spawned a tornado that crossed the Keys less than five miles away. The idea of a tornado ripping through Boot Key Harbor with all those people in their little boats is just too horrible to think about.

We also learned from this episode, improving our ground tackle by adding more chain to our anchor lines (to keep them more horizontal), and assembling and using sentinels (weights rigged to ride on the anchor line, holding it down for an even more horizontal pull on the anchor.)

~   ~   ~   ~   ~   ~   ~

Taken in its entirety, our Boot Key experience was simply outstanding. There was no question in my mind that I was a *very* lucky guy. I often said to people we met during the cruise, "do not pinch me—I do not want to wake up". Margaret's perspective on this is different, I am sure. What with cooking, cleaning up, hanging around laundry machines, schlepping groceries, and hauling up the anchor, it is a wonder she had the energy to write her ocassional newsletter piece. I was more than lucky . . . . I was *blessed!*

Margaret Speaks

THE VISIT FROM THE CHILDREN was wonderful. We celebrated our grandson Logan's fifth birthday on the beach at Sombrero Park with an exceptional birthday cake, complete with his favorite dinosaurs, from the local supermarket. Another day was taken up by a trip to Key West. Believe me, going by car and back in the same day was better rather than the four-day round trip by boat. We visited the aquarium, Ernest Hemingway's home, and other attractions, and watched the sunset among the crowds and magicians and jugglers.

On another day the group went out fishing on a party boat. I chose to stay on shore and baby-sit with our other grandson, Griffin. Ha ha ha! . . . as I predicted (quietly to myself), not a few of the gang got seasick. We also hung around the Faro Blanco pool at times, but the water was too COLD to enjoy swimming. *(Not for me – S.)*

Otherwise, I just hung in there, looking forward to the ports of call on the way home. Thank goodness for the book exchange libraries—all marinas have them. They range from a single shelf to entire bookcases containing paperbacks, hardcovers, and magazines. You browse and take what you want and bring in what you are finished with. I suppose the folks who go up and down the waterway each year see the same books bouncing from the Chesapeake to the Keys and back! I have been kept well supplied with my favorites: Margaret Truman, Agatha Christie, and Dick Francis.

Laundry areas at the marinas are great sources of information; not just gossip as Steve mentioned, but also useful info about water depths, changes in navigation aids, anchorages, and inside scoop on various marinas.

As far as the big storm goes, there's not much I can add to Steve's description except to note that he graciously left out the part where I goofed getting tied up in front of the condos. Steve did his usual good job in the high wind and surging waves in maneuvering the boat up to the pilings. He laid us right in there beautifully, and it was essential that we (me at the bow and he at the stern) get the dock lines secured to the pilings first shot. If you didn't, you'd have a problem because once you were in there you could be badly banged around against the steel bulkhead and the pilings.

Well, he got the stern tied up and I thought I had the bow secured . . . . but I didn't, and the line came undone. So we were tied at the stern and the bow was swinging and pitching wildly around into the channel. It took us another 15 minutes of trying to lasso the piling to get the situation tamed down. But we did it. This was a real partnership.

Hmmm . . . . . amen!

Aye, aye Sir!

8

Homeward Bound

Adios Dockside

A LL GOOD THINGS MUST come to an end, and so the days
were accomplished that we had to get the anchors up
and leave Boot Key Harbor.

Motoring over to the Marathon Boat Yard for
our haulout, I was sure there was something wrong with
the propulsion system because the boat seemed to have
difficulty moving and steering. With the boat out of the
water and hanging in slings at the boat yard, we soon
saw the reason—you simply would not believe the
amount of animal and vegetable life growing on the bottom
of this boat. The overall thickness was almost an inch—
barnacles, seaweed, small crustaceans, and colorful, bloby,
slimy critters. The shaft, propeller, rudder, everything
was smothered with this stuff. Fresh water sailors are
not accustomed to this. But anchor a boat for eight

weeks in a warm tropical lagoon, and this is what you get.

An hour later we were back in the water after being scraped and pressure-washed, our bottom clean and relatively smooth. I also installed a new sacrificial zinc on the shaft, having lost the old one in an unfortunate encounter with a fisherman's float and line on the way down the Keys. The debris from the boat's bottom, when shoveled up from the concrete pavement, practically filled a 30-gallon drum.

For our return trip to Miami we chose the inside route on the Florida Bay side of the Keys. After the first day's sail, as we were turning into an anchorage called Cowpens off Plantation Key, we noticed that the boat which had been traveling behind us was also turning in, and we saw that it was an Endeavor 42 center cockpit named *Uncle Harry.* We knew this boat and had last seen

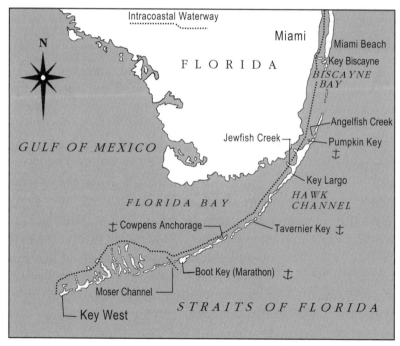

On the way home from Boot Key, we traveled on the Florida Bay side of the Keys, stopping at Cowpens, Jewfish Creek, and Miami.

it and it's skipper at Tidewater Marina in Havre de Grace, Maryland, at the top of Chesapeake Bay in August. We raised them on the VHF radio and were invited for sundowners in *Uncle Harry's* commodious cockpit. After we got the anchor down, Margaret rowed us over, because I didn't feel like hassling the outboard off the stern rail onto the dinghy. Rowing our undersized (and usually under-inflated) inflatable with two oversized (and usually over-inflated) people in it is like rowing a bathtub through mud, but Margaret, who volunteered for this, did a fine job.

Our visit with the *Uncle Harry's* skipper and mate was pleasant. It turned out that we have mutual friends in the Cleveland area. These folks live aboard *Uncle Harry;* their home base is Havre de Grace.

The Manatees of Jewfish Creek

U NCLE HARRY got off to an early start in the morning, so when we arrived at our destination the next afternoon, *Uncle Harry's* crew was there to help *Witch of Endor* into her slip. We stayed at the Anchorage Resort, which is a small condo/marina complex on Key Largo at the bottom of Jewfish Creek (a mile-long waterway through mangrove islands between Blackwater Sound and Barnes Sound).

A cold front with lousy weather kept us there for three days, which wasn't all that bad because the resort boasts a small but nice pool and jacuzzi, and there was a Chinese restaurant nearby that delivered to your boat. (*Yea!*)

But the real significance of this place on Key Largo is that it was the site of our first real manatee encounter. Manatees are huge, harmless vegetarian mammals that feed on underwater grasses and such. They are endangered and near extinction here in Florida, and there is much ado about preserving them. Their primary predator is the recreational boater, and their known habitats along the

Big, gentle vegetarians, manatees were once known as sea cows and were captured for meat. Cowpens anchorage at Plantation Key derives its name from this unfortunate practice. Photo courtesy of NASA.

waterways are zoned for slow speeds They are like big underwater cows, totally defenseless, and quite adorable. There are relatively few left in Florida (I think 2,000 or so) and many are numbered and/or named, and some carry radio transmitters so they can be tracked.

One afternoon there at the Anchorage Resort, two manatees appeared around the docks, one large—10 to 12 feet—and one smaller. The older, larger ones are brownish and the younger ones more gray. You see them as they surface for air and then you can follow them as they move underwater. They love fresh water, and if you direct the stream from a hose into the water, they will rise to it and drink. They will even hold the hose between their flippers to drink. I am told that their normal way of getting fresh water is through their skin by an osmosis process that excludes the salt. They will eat lettuce from your hand, and it is said that if you give them a head of lettuce, they will hold it in their flippers, rotating it like a giant squirrel eating an acorn. They are lovable critters.

Miami Sunset

L EAVING *UNCLE HARRY* behind at Key Largo, we had an easy day's run through Biscayne Bay up to Miami, where we anchored for the night in the old Marine Stadium. This is a wonderfully protected anchorage consisting of a long U-shaped harbor where water skiing shows used to take place, but it has not been used since Hurricane Andrew damaged the grandstands years ago. We watched the sun setting behind the Miami skyline across the bay while dining in the cockpit, and enjoyed the sparkle of the high rise office and apartment buildings after dark.

The next day we motored up condo alley to Fort Lauderdale, passing under 16 bridges, 11 of which needed to open for us. On our first night at Cooley's Landing we enjoyed a visit by Lake Erie dockmates, who were in Lauderdale pursuing their search for a live-aboard boat. They treated us to a wonderful shore dinner at Shirttail Charley's.

On St. Patrick's Day we enjoyed some brew while sitting by the river across from the Riverwalk Park, watching the never-ending parade of boats.

We stayed for a week and a half in Fort Lauderdale, enjoying the place the second time as much as we did during our first visit in December. We explored the Museum of Discovery and Science, where we were fascinated by a huge, two story Rube Goldberg water clock.

We also visited the Museum of Art, which was showing an exhibit of the late George Segal, the sculptor who created life-like human figures. We have some of his work in the Cleveland Museum of Art, and an outdoor piece at the State Office Building in downtown Cleveland. The Segal works that we had seen previously were monochrome in white or gray, but the figures in this exhibit were fully clothed and, you should pardon the expression, in living color. They were extremely life-like. When we first entered the gallery, we thought they were visitors

Left, the 17th Street Causeway Bridge, Fort Lauderdale. Right, Shirttail Charley's on the New River, where our Sandusky friends treated us to a wonderful shore dinner. Photos courtesy of Claiborne S. Young.

Sailboats anchored on the Indian River near Stuart. Photo courtesy of Claiborne S. Young.

like ourselves. These pieces attracted us. At first you wonder what they mean and why anyone would make them, but after a while they seem to grow on you.

We felt particularly drawn to a portly middle-aged couple, obviously tourists. She wore brightly colored slacks, a straw hat, rhinestone-studded harlequin sunglasses, and carried a colorful tote bag. He wore a loud sports shirt hanging out over his pants and a pork pie hat. He had a camera hanging around his neck, and the stub of a cigar clamped in his mouth. We stood there wondering why we felt such an affinity with these dumpy fake people, but soon we realized: *they were us!*

Northward to Vero Beach

A FTER TWO BEAUTIFUL (but windy) days of motorsailing and two pleasant nights at anchor, we arrived at Vero Beach. This is a popular place with cruisers—we had stayed there briefly on the way down, and planned to spend some time there on the way back.

Vero Beach boasts a nice municipal marina and mooring basin in a park-like setting, and great facilities including an extensive library and a comfy TV lounge. The marina is a pleasant walk from the Atlantic beach and Boca/Palm Beach type shops and restaurants (but not as expensive). Moreover, it is a short bus ride from supermarkets, a Wal-Mart, and other stores.

The Waterway markers at the entrance to the marina and mooring basin (it is kind of tucked around behind an island) were changed since we were there on the way down, and because of this, we went seriously aground trying to get in. After many tricky maneuvers (including a serious talk with the boat about pride and destiny) we finally managed to get ourselves unstuck and thus avoided the embarrassment of a tow.

After staying at a dock for a couple of nights, we spent a week on a mooring (much cheaper). We walked to the beach for picnicking and swimming, we shopped, and we socialized with other cruisers, cockpit hopping at sundowner time. We were pleasantly surprised to find *Lady Ann* in the marina. She is a large pilothouse boat that we traversed the Erie Canal with on the way down. We had last seen her at Cape May, New Jersey.

A French boat was moored at Vero Beach. We first came across this boat a day or so before, somewhere around Jupiter Inlet and Hobie Sound. It was traveling north like us, and we were sort of helping it in speaking to the bridges because of what we perceived to be a language difficulty. It was a scruffy, homemade-looking steel sailboat of around 40 feet, flying the French flag. There was a young couple on board, with children. Chatting over laundry, Margaret learned that the husband had sailed the boat over from France with some friends (who then returned), and was joined by his family (wife and three children, ages five to nine), which had flown to

The fuel dock at Vero Beach Municipal Marina, left. Right, a view of the mooring basin. Fuel dock photo courtesy of Claiborne S. Young.

Florida. They were headed for New York, from where the wife and children were going to fly home. We got accustomed to seeing this family and their boat over the next week as we shared anchorages with them at Dragon Point and St. Augustine. We called them the Frenchies.

Watch That Dragon!

A FTER A PLEASANT EVENING anchored at the bottom of the Banana River behind Dragon Point, we spent two nights at the Titusville Municipal Marina, a night at Daytona, and two nights at the Palm Coast Resort Marina as we worked our way northward to St. Augustine. We enjoyed our first stopover there last fall and were looking forward to visiting again. But first, a few words about Dragon Point and Palm Coast.

Merritt Island lies between the Indian River (the route of the ICW) and the Banana River. The southern end of Merritt Island is a long skinny piece of land, coming to a point near Melbourne. On the tip of this point, where the islands very narrow, sits a 200-foot long statue of a green dragon, built there and

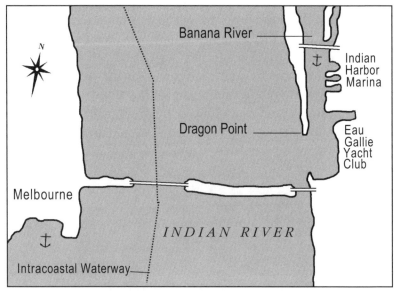

Dragon Point at the bottom tip of Merritt Island.

Here's a picture of the dragon. Around behind him and up the Banana River to the left, there is a delightful place to anchor for the night. The guy in the dinghy trying to hand a jerry can of water up to his wife is being seriously harrassed by a covey of curvaceous critters. Watch out, John . . . . here comes another one! Dragon photo courtesy of Claiborne S. Young.

maintained by the owners of the property. Talk about landmarks . . . *this* is a landmark.

Tucked in behind Dragon Point there are several marinas and a very nice anchoring area. Our enjoyment of the evening we spent there was enhanced by a pod of playful porpoises cavorting among the anchored boats. The skipper of a sailboat near us was replenishing his water by making trips ashore with jerry cans in his dinghy. When he was alongside his boat, trying to hand the cans up to his mate, the frisky critters would surface between the dinghy and the boat, to the extreme annoyance of the skipper, who almost got a dunking. But everyone else, including his mate and the splashing, chirping porpoises, thought it great sport.

The Palm Coast Marina is part of the Palm Coast Resort, which includes the Harborside Inn with restaurants and full tennis and golf facilities. I mention this because, like the Sheraton Grand Hotel and Marina in New Bern, North Carolina, cruisers staying at the marina have full access to the hotel amenities. Our stay at Palm Coast was special because of the enjoyment we derived from the beautifully landscaped grounds and pool, and the well-stocked Ship's Store, where we were able to pick up some nice gifts. In addition, we had the pleasure of meeting Bessie, the manatee.

The marina at Palm Coast and a shot of the Waterway nearby. This is typical of the Waterway through Northern Florida. Photos courtesy of Ida Hallerbach.

I was sitting under the awning at the cockpit table working on the laptop on a gorgeous sunny Palm Sunday afternoon when Bessie was sighted in the marina. She is about 12 feet long, and looks as if she must weigh over 1200 pounds. She wears a radio transmitter permanently strapped to her back. You can see the little antenna sticking up out of the water when she swims near the surface.

A couple of years ago Bessie was found near Boston Massachusetts in the wintertime, and was brought back home to Florida by Marineland. She's kept track of pretty closely now. No one knows why Bessie headed north. Maybe she had a hankerin' for some of those baked beans (for a quicker motion through the ocean).

~   ~   ~   ~   ~   ~

On arriving at St. Augustine, we anchored north of the Bridge of Lions, just off downtown and the 16th century Spanish fort, Castillo de San Marcos. This is a short dinghy ride to the Municipal Marina and its dinghy dock. Checking out the marina, we saw Skybird, a Ranger 33 whose home dock was across the way from ours in Sandusky. No one was home, so we left a note in the cockpit.

St. Augustine charmed us again as we walked the town the next day, touring various historic sites and taking pictures of the fabulous Henry Flagler buildings.

The Bikers

FERNANDINA BEACH is the northernmost city on Florida's East Coast. It is on Amelia Island, the first of the great Sea Islands that stretch northward along the coast through the Low Country of Georgia and South Carolina up to Charleston. Cumberland, Jekyll, St. Simon's, Sapelo, St. Catherine's, Ossabaw, Tybee, Hilton Head, St. Helena, and Kiawha are among the better known.

The Sea Islands are low and marshy, but rich in plant and animal life. After the Civil War, freed slaves took over the land of the abandoned plantations. Living in relative seclusion, these people, known as the Gullah, developed a unique culture and language based on African and English influences. This proud heritage endures today in the region.

There is a good anchorage directly across the Waterway channel from the Fernandina Harbor Marina, and we had planned to anchor there for a couple of days, using the dinghy to get ashore. After the first night at anchor, however, strong winds and choppy water prevented use of our little dinghy, and since the winds were forecasted to continue for several days, we moved to a dock in the marina.

The marina provides bikes for transients to use, so we donned our backpacks and biked across town to Walmart's and a supermarket for groceries and supplies.

This is Charlie. He followed us all the way from Boot Key Harbor.

We also filled a propane tank, had a great shepherd's pie shore dinner at our Irish pub, and toured the pretty downtown on foot. Fernandina Beach was fun.

The next day was Easter Sunday. We attended the 9 AM service at historic St. Peter's Fernandina and got away from the dock by noon—destination: Jekyll Island, Georgia. We made it past the King's Bay submarine base, and trekked on up behind Cumberland Island. After crossing St. Andrew's Sound (the track of the ICW across St. Andrew's takes you practically into the Atlantic), we tied up late Easter afternoon at the Jekyll Harbor Marina, where Margaret, bless her heart, prepared a marvelous Easter dinner. (Ham, potatoes *au gratin*, peas, and boat-made cookies for dessert. Wow!)

We relaxed that evening, looking forward to the next day's exploration of Jekyll Island. We were well on our way up the coast on our homeward journey, and we had many new adventures ahead of us.

Aw come on . . . I *did* the flies today.

Where the Pel'kins and Porpoises Play

I'll Meet You at the Club

JEKYLL ISLAND is an interesting place. In the 1880's a group of America's wealthiest men bought the island from the French family that had owned it since 1794 and developed it into a private resort. They formed the Jekyll Island Club and built a huge clubhouse together with a golf course and other facilities needed for a winter retreat. Limited to 100 members, the Jekyll Island Club was described in a 1904 edition of *Munsey's Magazine* as ". . . the richest, the most exclusive, the most inaccessible club in the world." It was open for the post-Christmas season, when the Astors, Vanderbilts, Morgans, Goulds, Rockerfellers, Cranes, Goodyears, Pulitzers, McCormicks and the other very wealthy families came down from Newport, New York, and Chicago on their sumptuous yachts or private railroad cars to get away from the nasty northern winters. (Snowbirds!)

The original Jekyll Island Club building is now a hotel. Photo courtesy of Jekyll Island Club Hotel.

The original idea was that the families would stay in the vast clubhouse, but members soon built their own "cottages"—enormous residences designed to house entire families and guests with complete staffs. Supposedly, these houses were built without kitchens or dining rooms, because meals were taken at the clubhouse.

This private preserve continued in full swing right up to 1942 when the U.S. government ordered the area evacuated, presumably because of the threat of German landings. The State of Georgia bought the island in 1947, built a causeway from the mainland, turned the clubhouse into a hotel, and created a magnificent public vacationland with controlled development of additional hotels, golf courses, tennis facilities, and other amenities.

The morning after our arrival, we rented bikes and spent a pleasant day exploring the island. We checked out the clubhouse (nice) and pedaled past some of the "cottages", many of which are restored and open for tours. We also biked beyond the historic district to get a look at the golf courses, hotels, and beaches.

That evening we dined at the marina cafe, gorging ourselves on Low Country Boil (shrimp, sausage, red skin potatoes, and corn on the cob—all you could eat for $11.95). This dish is also known as Froggmore Stew and Beaufort Stew, according to my brother Joe, who transplanted himself to South Carolina 20 years ago.

A Change for the Better

MARGARET'S CONTINUOUS ANXIETY about going aground was for me one of the minor annoyances on the voyage so far. We smooshed into the mud or sand from time to time—sometimes just powering through it, but most of the time getting stuck and having to back or wiggle out. Sometimes we hit hard, with the boat stopping abruptly, throwing the bow down and the stern up. It would happen for a variety of reasons: inattention or confusion on my part, shoal places not marked on the chart, channel markers not where they ought to be—whatever. Fortunately, only once did we get so badly stuck that we needed a tow.

Hitting the mud is no fun, and one does not do it on purpose. I am sure Margaret understood this, but her anxiety prompted frequent expressions of her displeasure at

Pukka on the bridge deck guarding goodies from our Easter mail package.

the way the boat was being steered, with the implication that the reason we hit the bottom (although it was rare that we did) was because I was not doing something right. Well, you can't be married for over 40 years without developing some immunity to this sort of thing, but it was irritating nevertheless.

Happily, all this changed in northern Georgia just south of Savannah in the Skidaway River, between the Skidaway Narrows Highway Bridge and Isle of Hope, not far from Johnny Mercer's Moon River. Margaret was at the helm, and she wandered out of the channel and ran us hard aground on a mud bank. Without going into all the details about how we got her off (I tried all my usual tricks to power her off, but she was _really_ stuck), for the first and only time on the entire voyage, *Witch of Endor* had to be towed off the ground.

It was a blessed miracle! How I wished it had happened sooner. Not once—never—from that April 15th afternoon to the day Pukka and I sit with two fingers and a paw pecking out these paragraphs—has the subject of going aground been raised in a manner suggesting fault. It sure made the rest of the trip more enjoyable.

Beaufort, South Carolina

A FTER A COUPLE OF delightful days winding northward through beautiful grassy marshes and crossing the sounds and rivers (and meeting *Nantucket Clipper* again, this time near Hilton Head Island), we tied up at the

Two of Beaufort's historic houses. The Thomas Fuller house, left, and the Milton Maxey house. Photos courtesy of CoastalGuide.com.

The esplanade along the riverfront park in Beaufort, with the Downtown Marina in the background. This is where *Nantucket Clipper* ties up.

Downtown Marina of Beaufort, in the heart of the Low Country. (This is "Bewfort", not to be confused with "Bowfort", North Carolina).

Beaufort is right on the river. The handsome 18th and early 19th century houses that line Bay Street look out over the marina docks and nearby anchorage, and the marina itself is adjacent to a nicely landscaped riverside park. To walk these quiet residential streets is to be transported back in time to the antebellum South. It is a shame that the word "beautiful" is so overworked, because it is the only word that adequately describes these wonderful houses and gardens set in the midst of magnificent, moss-laden oak trees. This is not a "restored" district in the sense that the houses are museums; lucky families live here.

We were actually in Beaufort for more than a week because of what we thought was a transmission problem—the boat didn't seem able get up to normal speed under power. The culprit turned out to be barnacles, and the boat was hauled at Marsh Harbor Boatyard (an excellent yard) for scraping and inspection of shaft and propeller. But this could not have happened in more congenial surroundings. We love Beaufort.

The Short Peoples' Church

ST. HELENA'S EPISCOPAL CHURCH in Beaufort is a wonderful old place. The parish was established in 1712 and the building was built in 1724. The first time that we went to

St. Helena's Episcopal Church, Beaufort, South Carolina. A tall Church for such short folks! Photo courtesy of CoastalGuide.com.

Church there (we spent a weekend in Beaufort on the way down), I had a strange experience. During the procession at the beginning of the service, it seemed to me that everyone was unusually short. The crucifer, the choir, the acolytes, the clergy—all were short. I asked myself, "Why is everybody so short?" Looking around, I saw that the congregation seemed to be of normal size. Just the people processing up the aisle were short. I puzzled about this during the service until the time came to go up for communion, when I *stepped down* into the aisle from the pew. I had forgotten that the pew floor level was raised up about eight inches from the floor level of the aisles. Oh, well. I felt short too.

Cockpit Talk—April 29: New Cut Landing to Price Creek

Margaret	Don't go between that green 77 and the shore—leave it to starboard.
Steve	No, I won't . . . the chart is clear about the shoal in there.
	Here we go . . . we're on our way! I see two greens ahead, then we kind of bend to the left.
Margaret	How's our depth?

Steve	OK . . . we're in 14 to 15.
Margaret	Can you see the red marker ahead?
Steve	No.
Margaret	See the second white area from the right just before the end of the tree line? The marker's on a dolphin.
Steve	Yeah . . . I've got it now. Boy, this river winds around.
Margaret	Favor the red side through here . . . chart shows shoaling on the other side.
Steve	Hey, here comes Charlie (*pelican*) . . . followin' us all the way from Boot Key . . . *hey, Charlie!*
	Look at the wake thrown by those pilings . . . we've got the current with us for a change. We're flyin' . . . what a great day! I'm a lucky fella . . . (*sings*) . . .

> *Oh give me a home . . .*
> *where the Manatee roam . . .*
> *and the Pel'kins and Porpoises play.*
>
> *Where seldom is heard . . .*
> *A discouraging word . . .*
> *And fried seafood is served all the day.*
>
> *Home . . . home on . . . the whataway . .*
> *where the Pel'kins and Porpoises play.*
> *Where seldom is heard . . .*
> *A discouraging word . . .*
> *and fried seafood is served ev'ry day.*

Steve	We've got a bridge ahead. What's its opening schedule?
Margaret	Looks like it's on demand.
Steve	What's its name?
Margaret	John F. Limehouse Highway Bridge.
Steve	OK.

Steve (radio)   *John F. Limehouse Bridge . . . John F. Limehouse Bridge . . . northbound sail vessel calling John F. Limehouse Bridge . . . come in please.*

Come on, Limehouse . . . let's go.

John F. Limehouse Bridge . . . hailing John F. Limehouse Bridge . . . over.

Bridge (radio)   *This is John Limehouse Bridge.*

Steve (radio)   *John Limehouse, this is a northbound sail vessel requesting an opening, over.*

Bridge (radio)   *Bring 'er on down, Cap'n and I'll be open when you get here. What's the name of your vessel, Cap'n?*

Steve (radio)   *Witch of Endor . . . that's EEE ENN DEE OOH ARE.*

Shoot, what's he waiting for . . . he hasn't even stopped the traffic yet.

There we go . . . there go the bells . . . gates are going down. Yeah . . . OK . . . gosh these swing jobs are slow.

Here we go.

Thanks, Limehouse . . . you have a nice day . . . Witch of Endor clear 'n standing by on 9 and 16.

Bridge (radio)   *Thank you Cap'n . . . y 'all have a nice trip.*

~   ~   ~   ~   ~   ~

Margaret   You've got two ranges ahead.

Steve   OK . . . front or back?

Margaret   The first one's a back.

Steve   Shoot . . . I hate these back ranges . . . yeah . . . I see the low marker . . . where's the back marker . . . there it is . . .I'll get on the range as we swing around the bend.

Margaret   It's a <u>very</u> narrow channel with shoaling on each side . . . you've <u>got</u> to stay on that range.

Our route from the anchorage at New Cut Landing up through Charleston Harbor to Price Creek.

Steve	OK . . . here we go.
Margaret	Immediately as you come off this range, you're going to pick up a front range. See the back marker up there . . . to the left of that clump?
Steve	Yeah . . . OK, but let me concentrate on this one first.

~   ~   ~   ~   ~   ~

| Steve (radio) | *Calling southbound tow at marker 24 . . . south-bound tow . . . come in please.* |

Tow (radio)	*Southbound.*
Steve (radio)	*Cap'n, this the northbound sail vessel comin' at you 'round the curve . . . port-to-port OK? . . . over.*
Tow (radio)	*Port-to-port's fine, Cap . . . thanks for calling.*

~   ~   ~   ~   ~   ~

Steve	I see 21 and 20 . . . and a green one way up there, must be 19.
Margaret	That's 19A . . . after that one you don't curve to the right with the river, but go straight across and pick up Elliott Cut to Wapoo Creek.
Steve	Wapoo Creek, Schwapoo Creek . . . what is it with these names . . .where's the entrance . . . I can't see the entrance to the cut . . . there it is . . . . . there's a red/green on the shore over there.
Margaret	That's right . . . leave it on your right.
Steve	How could leave it on my left? . . . it's on the shore.
	Here we go into Elliott Cut . . . wow! . . . look at that current! . . . we're barely movin' . . . it'll take a while to get through . . . this cut is so narrow . . . looks like we're only doing one or two knots over the ground.
	Look, it's fully bulkheaded . . . like the Point Pleasant Canal in New Jersey. Remember that?
Margaret	Yeah . . . listen, when we get out of this cut and get up Wapoo Creek . . . you've got the Wapoo Creek Bridge. . and then the Ashley River and Charleston Harbor.
Steve	The current at the Wapoo Bridge is supposed to be strong . . . but I'd sure rather have the current against us like this, goin' through the bridge.

~   ~   ~   ~   ~   ~

Steve (radio)	*Wapoo Creek Bridge . . . Wapoo Creek Bridge . . hailing Wapoo Creek Bridge . . . come in please.*

Bridge (radio)   *This is Wapoo Creek.*

Steve (radio)   *Wapoo Creek . . . this is a northbound standing by for your 11:30 opening . . . over.*

Bridge (radio)   *Roger, Cap'n . . . I'll be opening in 18 minutes.*

Steve (radio)   *Roger, Wapoo Creek . . . We'll let those southbound through first on account of the current . . . sail vessel Witch of Endor circlin' and standin' by on 9.*

~   ~   ~   ~   ~   ~

Margaret   Now listen . . . when you get up there under that high level bridge you'll be entering the Ashley River . . . first you've got a 3 . . . then a 1 . . . then you're going out to a red 4 and making a near 90 degree to the right to another 3, leaving it on your right. You're going down the Ashley and then right down the main ship channel out through Charleston Harbor.

Steve   OK . . . Wow! . . . look at Charleston . . . there's the Battery where we walked with Joe and Nancy last fall . . . there's those great Charleston houses lookin' out over the harbor.

Margaret   Now listen . . . stay on this course past that red-green BP up there 'til we're abreast of number 32, then steer a course of 090° true up to number 26 which we won't be able to see for a while because it's a couple of miles . . . these are all floaters out here.

Steve   OK . . . that'll be about 097° magnetic . . . look at that aircraft carrier over there . . . it's the *Yorktown* . . . a museum open to the public.

                 OK, here we go on 097° magnetic . . . I can see that buoy up there with the nakeds . . . what's its number again?

Margaret   Twenty six . . . now when you get there, steer 048° true to the ICW entrance . . . there's a Waterway red marker there and a front range to lead us in.

Steve   Hey . . . look how close we're goin' to Fort
             Sumter . . . and that's the open Atlantic out
             there!

      ~   ~   ~   ~   ~   ~

Steve   These long straight stretches can get boring . . .
             that's *Scud* up there . . . remember them ·from
             the anchorage last night?

Margaret   You going to pass him?

Steve   I don't know . . . we'll see when we get up there
             . . . hey, *wait a minute!* . . . this is getting really
             shallow . . . I'm getting 4's and 5's (5½ to 6½
             feet) . . . with jumps to 3 . . . *I don't like this at
             all* . . . when I get up there behind *Scud* I'm
             staying there. He needs more water than we do
             . . . we'll follow in his track and he can be our
             stalking horse.

*We made it up to Price Creek where we planned to anchor for
the night, and the next day had an easy run up to Winyah Bay
and Georgetown.*

Witch of Endor tucked in with the
shrimp fleet at Georgetown, South
Carolina.

Wrightsville Beach to Oriental

COAST GUARD ENCOUNTERS: We had a verbal boarding as we were cruising up the Waterway between Lockwood's Folly River and Southport just south of the Cape Fear River. A Coast Guard boat fell in close behind us and carried on a friendly but lengthy and exhaustive interrogation over the VHF radio. This was a deep interrogation—where have you been, where are you going, mother's maiden name, childrens names, everything. They also needed me to tell them information clearly visible on the stern of the boat, 12 yards in front of their noses, like name of vessel and homeport—as if an elderly man with his matronly wife and their scrawny cat were running a stolen boat!

We were not boarded, possibly because we had just experienced a joint (poor choice of words in the circumstances) boarding by the Coast Guard and the Florida Marine Patrol in Boot Key Harbor. The boat behind us got the same treatment, however, and *was* boarded. Later, in the Cape Fear River (we still _hate_ the Cape Fear River), we were subjected to hostile scrutiny by another Coastie patrol vessel. Oh well . . . . I guess we should be glad they were doing their job.

While anchored (with The Frenchies again!) in the wonderful anchorage at Wrightsville Beach, three Coasties visited all the boats in one of their rigid inflatables, warning of a very severe storm headed our way, and advising that a second anchor be set. One of the kids noticed our hailing port (Bay Village, OH) on our stern . . . it turned out that his aunt and uncle live not far from us, and keep their boat in Sandusky!

The storm was a humdinger, with 35 to 40 MPH winds and higher gusts . . . it was good that we put out that second anchor. We held our ground OK, but we had a real problem getting that anchor up in the morning. To this day I'm not sure what happened. Somehow, that second anchor line got wrapped around the keel, and in the still-strong wind, we couldn't budge the line. I had set

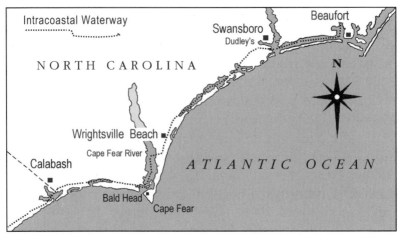

Coastal southern North Carolina. This is the section where the Waterway goes through the Marine Corps firing range at Camp Lejeune.

it by letting out a lot of line on the first anchor, then walking the second anchor (cleated at the bow) to the stern to drop it, and then taking back on the first line. It will snow in hell before I try that again. Because it was still very windy, we needed the help of a towboat to get us unwound and unanchored before we could get out of there.

A couple of days later, at Swansboro North Carolina, we had bad weather again. We were nailed down at Dudley's Marina for a couple of days, giving me the chance to work on the newsletter and do some engine maintenance. After leaving Dudley's, we had a good day's run up Bogue Sound, past Beaufort, and up the Adams Creek Canal and Adams Creek to a pretty anchorage in Cedar Creek, about three miles south of where Adams Creek joins the Neuse River.

The following morning it was raining and blowing. After getting the anchor up and motoring the three miles out of sheltered Adams Creek into the Neuse River, where it opens out into Pamlico Sound, we realized it was _not_ a good day to travel on open water. We crossed the river to Oriental, where we spent the rest of the day and evening anchored in the cozy little harbor at the marina entrance (see map on page 141).

Spending weather days in a snug anchorage is not an unpleasant experience. One works hard turning one's boat into a self-sufficient capsule with water, electricity, heat, radios, tapes, books, comfortable lighting, beer, wine, liquor, food (and a cook!)—everything that might be wanted in such a circumstance. Sometimes it is pleasant to just relax in the small world that you have created and can control, and let the outside world take care of itself.

Margaret Speaks

WELL, I NEVER THOUGHT I was quite in the same category as tapes, liquor, and electricity, but Steve continues to be so easy to please in the food department that I will forgive him. *(How modesty becomes you, my dear!).*

We enjoyed a return visit to Calabash North Carolina for—guess what? . . . fried seafood . . . *for <u>my</u> birthday dinner yet!* While we were at Dudley's, Steve, watching the incoming fishermen clean their catch on the dock during cocktail hour, traded one of his vodka specials for some beautiful just-caught dolphin (that's the fish—not Flipper. It's called Mahi Mahi on menus). He prepared it for us as part of a delicious Mother's Day dinner.

I'm still hangin' in there, looking forward to seeing Kerry and Joann when we get to Annapolis.

As far as going aground goes, I can only say that it was something that concerned me a lot.

Hmmm . . . .

10

The Story of Uncle Sam

The Final Days

WITH THE END of our adventure in sight, we were more conscious of the passing days. Our need to be in Sandusky by mid-July began to exert a gentle pressure—we no longer enjoyed the luxury of not worrying about the passage of time. The open-ended feeling that had characterized our journey up to this point was replaced by the realization that we would be home in a few weeks.

Margaret was anxious to get there, but my feelings were mixed. The approaching close of our escapade saddened me—returning to the dreary world of cutting the grass and taking out the garbage was not an exciting prospect. I was going to miss my Peter Pan life, leading my little vagabond band to new places and new adventures. I felt as if the end of the happy, carefree days was near, and of course, it was; waking up is not the best part of living a dream. Pukka, moping around the cabin with a hang-cat expression on her face, seemed to mirror my melancholy mood.

Nevertheless, we all looked forward to being home in the Hudson in a few weeks, and also to our trip across the Erie Canal. We had been through so much together since our first Erie Canal crossing that the prospect of locking *up* 570 feet westward across New York State did not faze us.

On our way up to the Chesapeake, we stayed again at River Forest Marina in Belhaven. One advantage we had on the return trip was that we could avoid the anchorages and marinas that were less than great on the way down, and stop again at the places we enjoyed. And there was no way that I could be within 50 miles of Belhaven, North Carolina without stopping to get some of those oyster fritters.

So we turned into River Forest (passing the Frenchies at anchor in Belhaven's little harbor!), and raced through the docking and clean up chores. In due course, stomach fluttering in anticipation, I approached the buffet table only to discover that there were no oyster fritters. *No oyster fritters!* What a letdown. I learned that the cook had simply decided not to have them that day. Was this right? Could cooks just go and *do* that? I was flabbergasted. Later, I sat down with the gentle Mrs. Smith and explained that the River Forest buffet was famous in Waterway literature for oyster fritters, that cruisers would stop by expecting to have them when oysters were in season, and that perhaps the cook should not have the latitude, etc. She listened quietly. What a gracious lady to put up with such nonsense!

The Neuse Goose

A FEW DAYS EARLIER, when we were in that pretty anchorage in Cedar Creek, I noticed a tidy little house on shore. It had a dock with an attractive blue-hulled trawler tied up to it. I said to myself, "This is some lucky person's shore base—what a great set-up!" Later, while truckin' up the Alligator-Pungo Canal, singing the Alligator-Pungo song (not worth memorializing here, or anywhere else, for that matter), we were passed by a blue-hulled trawler. That afternoon we shared an anchorage with it in Little Alligator Creek.

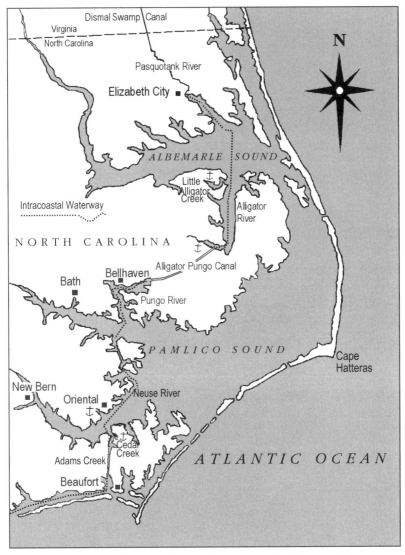

Map of coastal North Carolina showing the track of the Intracoastal Waterway and our Cedar Creek, Oriental, and Little Alligator Creek anchorages.

The next day, as we were crossing Albermarle Sound headed for the Pasquotank River and Elizabeth City on our way to the Dismal Swamp Canal, I noticed that the blue-hulled trawler was also crossing the Sound. She was headed in a more easterly direction, towards the entrance to the Albermarle and Chesapeake Canal, which is the alternate route to Norfolk at the bottom of the Chesapeake.

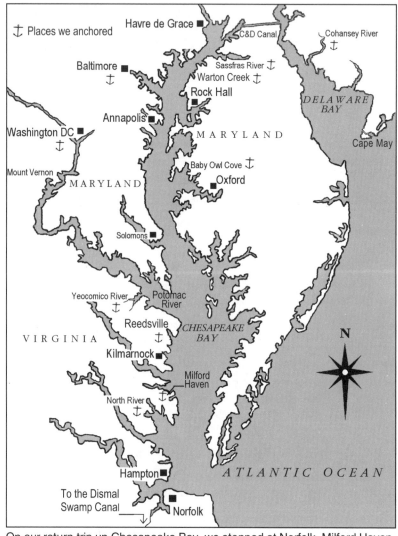

On our return trip up Chesapeake Bay, we stopped at Norfolk, Milford Haven, Reedsville, Solomons, Annapolis, Warton Creek, and the Sassafras River.

Our floating home snuggled down for the night at Milford Haven, behind Gwynn Island, in the Chesapeake. Photo courtesy of William McIntyre, *Neuse Goose.*

When we got to Waterside Marina in Norfolk several days later, after stopping in Elizabeth City and transiting the Dismal Swamp Canal, the blue-hulled trawler was there. (The Frenchies were there also, across the river in the Hospital anchorage!) As you've guessed, it was the same boat I noticed tied up at its dock in Cedar Creek. Its name is *Neuse Goose* and her Skipper and Mate live in that tidy little house with the dock when they are not cruising in the *Goose.* We traveled together for a couple of days up the Chesapeake, sharing anchorages and sundowners at Milford Haven and Reedsville, after which we parted company, with *Neuse Goose* going to St. Mary's while we headed for Solomon's, on our way up to Annapolis (passing the Frenchies, of course!).

Chesapeake Redux—or Racing Through Paradise

WE WERE IN THE CHESAPEAKE for only ten days, three of them spent in Annapolis over Memorial Day weekend. Kerry and Joann came down from their home in Reston, Virginia to visit us there, bringing the things we left with them on the way down in the fall.

Left, we are truckin' up the Chesapeake, passing the Windmill Point light which marks the Rappahannock Spit at the mouth of the Rappahannock River. This shoal extends about three miles off the Virginia shore. Right, hunkered down at Solomons Island in the Patuxent River, where we lucked into an incredible fried seafood buffet. Truckin' photo courtesy of William McIntyre, *Neuse Goose.*

Annapolis is the boating hub of Chesapeake Bay, and a wonderful place for boating people, particularly for sailboating people. We had a great holiday weekend. So, I expect, did the Frenchies, who we saw anchored there as we picked our way through the crowded harbor to get to our marina near the Spa Creek Bridge.

Although we ran the Chesapeake much too quickly, it nevertheless managed to cast its spell, producing verse two of the cockpit song, to wit:

> *Oh give me a home . . .*
> *where the Oystermen roam . . .*
> *in their skipjacks and boots all the day.*
>
> *Where seldom is heard . . .*
> *a discouraging word . . .*
> *from the Watermen workin' the Bay.*
>
> *Home . . . home on . . . the Ches'peake . . .*
> *where the yachtsmen and landlubbers play.*
> *Where seldom is heard . . .*
> *a discouraging word . . .*
> *they have oysters and crab ev'ry day.*

Cape May

AFTER LEAVING THE TOP of the Chesapeake and crossing the C & D Canal to the Delaware River, we spent a night in the Cohansey River, where we anchored last year on our way south. We then had a boisterous ride down

Delaware Bay to the Cape May Canal, where we holed up in Cape May waiting for high winds and seas to subside before going off shore and up the Jersey coast.

Cape May is an old-time seaside resort dating back to the mid-1800's. It is full of history, Victorian style hotels and houses, and tourists. After a night at anchor by the Coast Guard Station, we moved to a marina for two days of fun. We backpacked Cape May, exploring and shopping both by bike and on foot, including biking out to the Cape May lighthouse.

It was pleasant to stroll the streets of B&B's, pretty Victorian style houses ("painted ladies") all decked out with a profusion of wildly colorful flowers in window boxes and hanging baskets. The beach at Cape May is wide and beautiful, with several huge old Victorian style hotels looking out over the ocean. Cape May was well worth the visit.

Finally, in Cape May we come to the end of the saga of the Frenchies, which began on central Florida's sunshine coast. We found them anchored at Cape May when we arrived, and we dropped the hook right next door, near the Coast Guard Station. They were heading out the next morning for New York, from where the family was going to

Cape May scenes: left, one of the many gorgeous Victorian style "painted ladies". Right, a vast, sun-drenched hotel, facing the ocean across the wide, white sand beach.

Clockwise from upper left: the Frenchies' boat anchored at Cape May, the family returning from a shore excursion, Coast Guard cutters at Station Cape May.

fly home, with the father planning to single-hand the rust bucket back across the Atlantic. (Note that *we* were lingering in Cape May, waiting for high winds and seas to subside before venturing out—what a difference in style! But then, we're just a couple of old softies.)

New York at Last!

S COOTING UP THE JERSEY COAST, we stayed at Trump's Marina in Atlantic City, where we once again enjoyed one of those great casino buffet dinners.

One feature of Trump's that I had not seen at Harrah's the year before was a track betting room. It was softly lighted at a low level and furnished with luxurious black leather lounge seating and low tables arranged living room style. Numerous television monitors flickered in the surrounding shadows. I guess you could relax in there, and watch and place bets on any race at any track in the country, if not the world. What a life!

Before returning to the boat for the evening (we are not casino people), we made some routine check-in calls to our kids, including our daughter. She is a horse person who was a professional jockey in her youth (sorry, Pam!), and now operates a thoroughbred training business on the West Coast. When she heard where we were, she gave me the name of a horse about to run in the fifth at Longacres, the Seattle track, and told me to place a bet. Well . . . . . I didn't. Not only did I lack the right stuff to go and place the bet, but I was also too chicken to find out how the horse ran. Now you know, folks. Do not think *for a minute* that you could not do this trip. Believe me—if *I* can do it, _anybody_ can!

Underway again, in a couple of days we rounded Sandy Hook and sailed serenely under the Veranzzano Narrows Bridge into New York Harbor. Although it was our second visit to these waters in a year, it was still exciting for this plain, ordinary Midwestern couple to sail through the harbor, past the Statute of Liberty, and the Battery. It also was homecoming time again, this POMC (plain, ordinary, etc.) having lived and worked for so many years in the New York area.

We spent the night at a marina on the Jersey side of the Hudson opposite the World Trade towers. It was within sight of 17 Battery Place, where Margaret worked on an upper floor in our early days, when we lived in Brooklyn while I was in architectural school. She would have been able to look out of the window and see herself down there in the cockpit of *Witch of Endor* (if such a 40-year time warp were possible), but not knowing she was out there, she didn't look.

From the Newsletter, June 12: Rain in the Hudson

WE ARE MOST OF THE WAY up the majestic Hudson at Catskill NY, waiting our turn for our mast to be unstepped for our transit of the Erie Canal. Two days from when we leave here, we will be in the canal, savoring those lazy summer days while working our way westward across upper New York State. We'll be locking through the 35 locks required to raise us to the level of Lake Erie, and enjoying the wonderful hospitality of the canal towns along the way. Can't wait!

On our way up here to Catskill, we stopped for a couple of days at one of our old haunts from the trip south last year— Kingston City Dock on Roundout Creek. This is where we had to choose between Chinese and Japanese for dinner one night. Well, this time we chose Japanese, and it was good. But here's the joke: the same family owns both restaurants. I forget their name . . . probably Kowalski.

Sunday, June 14 Rain, rain, rain. We are still on Catskill Creek, tied up at Riverview Marine Services, unable to move on because of weather. We arrived here on Thursday, our mast was pulled on Friday, and yesterday morning we were squared away and ready to go

We were back in home territory, enjoying the Hudson and looking forward to the Erie Canal. Three days of rain caused the canal to shut down due to heavy debris, and we were holed up in Catskill Creek and Castleton waiting for the canal to open.

with our rig all secured on deck, but it has been *pouring* rain since Friday and the forecast is for more of the same today.

Our next stop after leaving here (tomorrow, we fervently hope) will be the Troy Town Docks, where we will do some shopping (like many marinas, there is a car for use by transients), and get this newsletter copied and mailed. Then, the day after that—the *Erie Canal!*

Wednesday, June 17 Well, we are at the Troy Town Docks all right, but we spent the last two days at Castleton-on-Hudson, which is between here and Catskill. The reason for our delay now is not the weather, which is fine. But the three-day heavy downpour wreaked havoc with the canal, and the locks at this end have been closed because they were jammed with tree trunks, branches and other debris. Motoring up the Hudson from Catskill, we had to keep a sharp lookout for the many partially submerged logs and tree trunks racing downstream with the current. Running into one of those babies would have brought our adventure to a swift, watery end. Remember: the Hudson has the deepest water we experienced on the trip.

Castleton-on-Hudson is just a couple of hours below Troy—we sat it out there because Troy was backed up with boats waiting for the locks to open. They are open now, so we will be heading out of here in the morning—*finally!*

The Story of Uncle Sam

NOW WE GET TO Uncle Sam. I recognize that many readers are familiar with this story, but I first learned it when we explored downtown Troy after we finished shopping and got everything stowed away. If you know this story, bear with me; I'll keep it short.

Sam Wilson was a businessman in Troy who held a contract to supply meat to the army during the

War of 1812. Each barrel of meat rations was stamped *US* before it was shipped to the soldiers. Sam Wilson became known to the troops, who affectionately referred to him as *Uncle Sam* Wilson, which they related to the *US* stamped on the barrels. They would say things like (so the story goes) ". . *hey! . . . here's another shipment from Uncle Sam!"*

Of course, we can only speculate about what the soldiers *really* thought of the salted meat in the barrels. But this story is important to the good folks of Troy— there's a statute, a park, and all sorts of memoralia (don't bother to look it up; it's a new word)—and so we will happily assume the best.

The most familiar image of Uncle Sam (the top-hatted gent wagging his finger at you) first appeared on recruiting posters during World War I. In 1961, the 87th US Congress adopted this resolution:

> *"Resolved by the Senate and House of Repre-sentatives that the Congress salutes Uncle Sam Wilson of Troy, New York, as the progenitor of America's National symbol, Uncle Sam."*

Margaret Speaks

I HAD NOT BEEN looking forward to the days when we would be crossing the Pamlico and Albemarle Sounds and the three days on the Atlantic Ocean, but as usual the anticipation was far worse than the reality. Anyway, we are now in the beautiful, serene Hudson and in familiar territory known from our New York days. I am looking forward to our journey along the Erie Canal, in spite of the chores of locking through.

The cooking, cleaning and laundry continues, and like another cruising wife I met, I will *kiss* my dishwasher when I get home! Meanwhile, tomorrow:

> *I've got a mule an' her name is Sal . . .*
> *Fifteen miles on the Erie Canal.*

Can't wait!

11

The Last Hurrah

The Music Barge

THE AFTERMATH of the heavy rains slowed us down a bit as we ascended the "Waterford Flight" and worked our way westward towards Schenectady. As we expected, locking up is more work that locking down, but we were pros and we did just fine. There was still a lot of floating debris in the canal, and we had to wait while some of the locks were cleared out by work crews in their nifty little blue and yellow tugs and barges. The New York State Canal Corporation (a subsidiary of the New York State Thruway Authority) does a great job maintaining this wonderful asset.

The eastern section of the canal runs in the Mohawk River, which winds westward through the Mohawk Mountains. They are gentle, old mountains—hills, really, their upper slopes checkered with bright, green pastures and darker woodlots. The barns and silos of dairy farms on the high distant hillsides sparkled in the sunshine chasing the cloud shadows across the slopes.

Down in the lowland, the canal shares the river valley with the New York Thruway (I-90) on one side and the main New York to Chicago railroad line on the other, and there are places where these are quite close by. A wave to an Amtrak locomotive brought an answering blast, and later we received an unsolicited friendly toot and wave from a Conrail freight locomotive. We also got a honk and wave from a passing Wal-Mart 18-wheeler truckin' across I-90. I guess an elderly couple and a cat pokin' along in a little boat with its mast lying on its deck was something to honk and wave at.

We passed a strange boat on this stretch of the canal, near St. Johnsville. It was a long, sleek craft that appeared to be made of stainless steel or aluminum. It was broad, low, and futuristic-looking. We didn't know what it was—until we got to Ilion, NY, where we stopped for fuel.

At the Ilion marina there was a sign announcing a concert by the American Waterways Wind Orchestra that had occurred there the previous week. We learned that the 195-foot stainless steel, self-propelled barge cruised the canal, and other waterways, giving free symphony orchestra concerts. It ties up to the shore, and with built-in hydraulic lifts, raises its 75-foot wide stage backed by a folding acoustical shell.

The orchestra is comprised of 45 young professional musicians from all over the US and around the world, who stay with local families during the orchestra's visit, which lasts several days. The musicians are paired with local kids who study the same instruments, and they provide private instruction and encouragement. Chamber music workshops are held for middle and high school musicians. *Five thousand people* attended the Ilion concert!

The barge, which is named *Point Counterpoint II*, travels the waterways of the East Coast and Gulf Coast, from New England to Mobile, Alabama. It plies the Intracoastal Waterway, and the Hudson, Ohio, Tennessee, and Tombigbee Rivers. Its home base is believed to be Pittsburgh, and it is also thought to have traveled the waterways of Europe. I found this to be an amazing story, and I vowed to find out more about it when I got home.

Schoharie Crossing

AT SCHOHARIE CROSSING there is an historic site with a number of canal artifacts and a two-mile self-guided canal and nature tour. We had spent the night at nearby lock 12, and since it was a wonderful sunny, mid-June day, we packed a picnic lunch and walked the tour.

Today's Erie Canal is different from the one first completed in 1825. That one was four feet deep and 40 feet wide. It was a huge success and had a tremendous impact on the development of the Northeast, Great Lakes, and Midwest regions. In 15 years it took New York City from 11th place in shipping tonnage, well behind Boston, Philadelphia, Baltimore, and New Orleans, to first place, shipping more than those cities combined.

The canal was enlarged and deepened in the 1840's and 50's, and then totally relocated and rebuilt between 1905 and 1918. As a result of these stages of development, there are distinctly different remnants—parts of the original "Clinton's Ditch" (after the visionary New York Governor DeWitt Clinton, who was responsible for the building of the first canal), and remnants of the later, enlarged canal.

During the walking tour we viewed a lock and about a half-mile of the original canal, and also a lock from the enlarged canal. The largest artifact at Schoharie Crossing is the remains of the Schoharie Aqueduct, which carried the water of the enlarged canal over and separate

Canal scene: we were a motor vessel again.

from the water of Schoharie Creek. It was more than 600 feet long when completed in 1842; seven of the fourteen original arches still stand.

One of the interesting technical points about all this is that the original canal was a man-made cut all the way from the Hudson River to Buffalo, running alongside naturally occurring waterways like, for example, the Mohawk River. The canal of today, which is the total rebuild of 1905-1918, makes maximum use of rivers and lakes all the way to Rochester. West of Rochester it runs in a man-made land cut to a point near Lockport, where it picks up the Tonawanda Creek to the Niagara River just north of Buffalo.

Reprise: Oh, Those Lazy Summer Days

SYLVAN BEACH is on Lake Oneida where the canal enters its eastern end. We spent an evening tied up there. It is a pleasant little resort village that, in addition to a beach, boasts an amusement park complete with rides, arcades, a midway, and a dance hall. It is family vacation oriented, and a 1950's kind of town. A slight aura of having been passed by—an air of respectable seediness—permeates the place. We loved it and felt right at home. I guess it brought back the beaches, the carnivals, and the Coney Islands of our long ago childhoods, when June nights smelled of excitement and promise.

We ate at Eddie's Restaurant where for 60 years Eddie and Florence (Fifi) Stewart and their children and now their grandchildren have served great food (if this can be extrapolated from our meals) to all comers. We were seated by Eddie's daughter-in-law, who assured us as we left that Eddie still came to the restaurant almost every day, and that Fifi was in the kitchen as we spoke.

According to the back of the menu, and there's no reason to doubt it, in days of former splendor when Sylvan Beach was known as the "Playground of Central New York" (locally, at least), Eddie's customers included the likes of Frank Sinatra, Duke Ellington, the Dorsey brothers, Desi Arnaz, Harry James, and the Ink Spots.

The canal dumps into the eastern end of Oneida Lake at Sylvan Beach and picks up again at the western end. The buoys that mark the 20-mile route across the open lake are placed about a mile apart, which is fine in clear weather but problematic when visibility is poor. There was fog over the lake the next morning, but we made the 4-hour crossing without mishap because we had the coordinates of one of the last buoys in the series, which provided us with a GPS waypoint. We also set out just behind a couple of trawlers, which gave us objects bigger than buoys to spot ahead, and visibility improved later in the morning.

Eddie's Restaurant in Sylvan Beach offered friendly service and good food. Sylvan Beach also featured a good triple-B tie-up wall: waste Barrels, Bollards, and Benches.

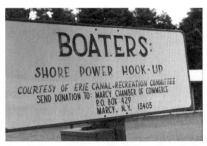

Left, Margaret takes her ease in the hammock at Ess-Kay Yards in Brewerton. Right, this sign demonstrates the hospitality of the towns along the Canal.

You DO Get Bread with One Meatball!

BACK IN THE CANAL, we tied up at Ess-Kay Yards at Brewerton, which is an outstanding marina. It's a pretty spot, nicely landscaped with shaded lawns sporting picnic tables and a comfy hammock. There are groceries and laundry facilities nearby, and the Ess-Kay ship's store is unusually well stocked with a wide variety of products. The staff is friendly and accommodating. We had a very pleasant stay there.

We stopped at Lyons to pick up mail and Father's Day packages (the Postmistress remembered us from the year before!), and to put down a serious Quarter Pounder attack—there's a McD's right there where you can sit under shade trees observing the locking activity while putting away the fries.

After Lyons, we drifted lazily across western New York, stopping at the towns we enjoy so much— Fairport, Spencerport, Brockport, Middleport. With their friendly bridge and lock tenders, their grassy, shaded places to tie up for the evening, and their downtown areas right there for easy exploring and shopping—each visit was a step through the looking glass back to small town America.

At Middleport, I walked into a little place just a stone's throw from the boat to get some ice, and noticed on the menu board that the specials on Tuesday were:

Spaghetti with bread and butter $1.75

Spaghetti with bread and butter,
one meatball and salad $2.75

Spaghetti with bread and butter,
two meatballs, and salad $3.25

I looked around and saw that the place was full of people
eating spaghetti. It was Tuesday. I went to get Margaret. It
was *good!*

Th . . Th . . Th . . That's All Folks!

W̶E FINALLY MOTORED serenely into Tonawanda, the
western terminus of the Erie Canal on the Niagara
River north of Buffalo, where we stepped the mast at
Wardell's and rigged the boat. Heavy rain then nailed us
down at the Buffalo Yacht Club for three days, but we
were soon working our way westward along Erie's
southern shore.

   We were so close to the July 4th fireworks display
at Dunkirk NY, that burnt particles rained down on the
foredeck as we watched the show from our cockpit at the
Dunkirk Yacht Club. It was a spectacular display, made
even more exciting by being so close. Erie, Ashtabula,
Fairport, and Cleveland were our next ports of call. We did
not stop at Lorain because we couldn't remember the
name of that damned bridge.

   On a Sunday afternoon, exactly one year and a
day after she left, *Witch of Endor* pulled into a slip at our
marina in Sandusky Bay, 50 miles west of Cleveland.
Some of the same dockmates who had partied with us so
boisterously the summer before were there to welcome us.

   We were home.

Stewart and Ellen had put our car in the marina lot for us, so we packed it with the first of what would be many loads. When Margaret opened the kitty carrier on the saloon table, Pukka jumped right in. She knew she was going home. And when we got into our house, she acted as if she had never been away, except for a slight roll in her gait.

Walking into our house was a pleasure—A/C on, everything neat and clean, fresh flowers everywhere, hot water and freezer on, and food in the refrigerator. Our kids and our friends had done a wonderful job of making our homecoming a joy.

Dorothy said it best. . there's no *place like home.*

Margaret Gets the Last Word

WELL, KISS MY DISHWASHER . . . . home at last! I know everyone will be anxious to learn if I had a good time, and whether I would want to do it again. Well, there were some days that were strenuous and uncomfortable, but I think that the most difficult thing for me was dealing with the uncertainties and unknowns inherent in an experience like this. Concerns about going aground, not knowing where we were going to be, going into unfamiliar harbors and marinas, anxiety about the weather . . . all these were stressful for me. So, I do not think I am ready to do this again.

But, having said all that, I will *also* say that the cruise was a wonderful adventure, and that I'm truly glad I did it and to have been a member of Steve's vagabond band. Nevertheless, Steve owes me . . . . BIG TIME !

(Hmmm . . . . . what does this *portend?)*

Coda

Margaret and Steve enjoying departure day festivities.

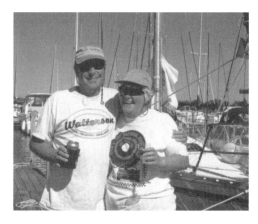

Margaret and Steve arriving home one year and a day later.

Pukka helping to write the book.

APPENDIX: The dull stuff

Finances

I believed it was important to set up a monthly budget for the cruise consisting of the actual cash outlays that we would be making during the trip, and that this budget should be kept separate from the ongoing expenses related to our home and other aspects of our lives. Accordingly, I set up a dual budget system involving two separate checking accounts, adjusting the inflows to the accounts to accommodate the needs of the budgets. This was possible because our income was derived from five separate direct deposits from sources such as Social Security, pensions, and annuities. In addition, between us we had three checking accounts.

Because of the uncertainty and irregularity of receiving mail on the go, I did not want to get and have to pay home bills while in Paradise. I wanted to be able to deal only with the expenses of the cruise itself, and so I set things up so that our son, Stewart, could manage the home budget.

The reason for segregating the budgets into separate checking accounts was to avoid a situation in which Stewart and I would both be drawing funds from the same account.

Canceling insurance on the cars minimized home expenses, along with dropping cable service and reducing phone service to vacation status. The house and boat mortgage payments were already being made by automatic withdrawal, as were life insurance payments. We further simplified the home bill-paying chore by putting utility payments on automatic withdrawal as well. We were able to forecast with fair accuracy what bills Stewart would be paying out of the home checking account over the course of the year. Boat insurance was paid as part of the home budget. (Boat insurance is discussed separately).

With respect to cruise expenses, I did not want to use a credit card as the vehicle for paying our day-to-day expenses and raising cash, because, again, I did not want to rely on the vagaries of our mail forwarding arrangements to receive the credit card bills. I wanted a way to raise cash and pay expenses as we went, without involving credit cards, mail, or personal checks.

The answer was to use a bank debit card (on the cruise budget checking account) that has the Visa symbol on it. This type of card is accepted as a credit card everywhere, the difference being that the charge is paid directly from the checking account and never shows up on a credit card bill. And, of course, it can be used to withdraw cash from the checking account at any ATM machine.

Our monthly budget for cruise expenses was $1,660, initially broken down as follows:

PLAN MONTHLY BUDGET

Food, Groceries, Miscellaneous		270.00
Shore Meals, Entertainment	3 per week @ 35	452.00
Dockage	4 per week @ 42	722.00
Pump Out	2 per week @ 10	86.00
Diesel Fuel	5 days x 8hrs x .45gal/hr x 1.30	100.00
Canal & Misc. Fees, Emergencies		30.00
	Total	1,660.00

Also indicated above are some of the assumptions used to develop the numbers. For example, for the monthly cost of fuel:

Assumes we would motor an average of five days out of seven for 8 hours a day at an average fuel consumption of .45 gallons per hour times assumed average cost of 1.30 per gallon times 4.3 weeks per month.

After a few months, it became apparent that, although the overall total was workable, the distribution among categories was out of whack. Food and Miscellaneous was closer to 450.00, Dockage was closer to 500.00, and fuel more like 50.00. Emergency expenses such as engine repairs, haulout and bottom cleaning, replacing lost anchors, and unexpected electrical and plumbing work were underestimated. (Some of this was put on a credit card and swept under the rug for Stewart to find)

ACTUAL MONTHLY BUDGET

Food, Groceries, Miscellaneous	450.00
Shore Meals, Entertainment	360.00
Dockage	500.00
Pump Out	50.00
Diesel Fuel	50.00
Canal & Misc. Fees, Emergencies	<u>250.00</u>
Total	1,660.00

This budget was OK but if I were doing it again, I'd look for another $200 a month for a little more wiggle room—but then all budgets are onerous, especially for Peter Pans leading vagabond bands.

The Boat

Witch of Endor is a Jeanneau SunLight 30, a light displacement, 30-foot sloop, built in 1986 in France. Being a sailboat, her primary motive power is the wind. Her auxiliary engine is a two-cylinder Yanmar® diesel. We bought her new in 1990.

She was equipped with 26 gallons of water tankage, which I increased to 50 to 60 gallons by installing a bladder (collapsible tank) under the saloon settee. While this is a good location from the plumbing stand point, adding all that weight so far off the centerline causes a 3 degree list to starboard when the tanks are full. Not at all pretty, but when the boat is at rest I can easily tell when the tanks are getting empty.

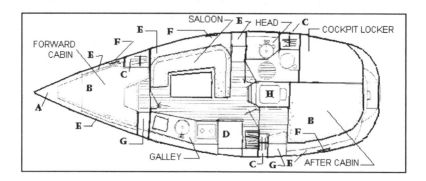

BELOW DECK ACCOMMODATION PLAN OF *WITCH OF ENDOR*

A	Pukka's Refuge	**E**	Shelf
B	Berth, Storage Under	**F**	Porthole
C	Hanging Locker	**G**	Clothes Locker
D	Navigation Station	**H**	Engine

I also added three batteries, making a total of four. I designated one of the four as the emergency engine starting battery. The three batteries comprising the house bank are connected in parallel to provide a theoretical 300 amp-hours. I installed a battery charger so that all batteries are charged when the boat is plugged into shore power.

The boat was equipped with an icebox. I installed a conversion kit transforming it into a refrigerator. I did not originally plan to do this, and this turned out to be the single most important modification I made. Don't even think about living for an extended period on a boat without refrigeration. The refrigerator runs off the batteries.

I had a catalytic propane heater installed in the saloon, the kind of heater that does not produce carbon monoxide and therefore does not require venting. We carried an excellent little electrical heater to use when we were plugged into shore power, and the propane heater was for use when we were at anchor. We didn't need it very much, but it was great to have when we did.

The teak magazine racks sold in the boating supply stores work very well for storing chart books and folded charts. I

View of the saloon looking towards the settee and the radio/tape player/TV shelf.

Looking forward from the saloon into the forward sleeping cabin. The galley is on the left.

The galley, with the forward cabin beyond. The refrigerator is top loading, and is located under the counter to the right of the sink.

Looking aft towards the after sleeping cabin. The navigation station is tucked behind the door to the aft cabin, right, and the companionway steps up to the cockpit and the door to the head are to the left.

The navigation station.

(These photos pre-date the cruise, so they don't show the interior precisely as it was on the trip. The picture of the cabin on page 94 is up-to-date.)

installed three of them (on doors), including one handy to the companionway for storing the hand-held VHF radio, the air horn, and the binoculars when these items were not in the cockpit.

To address concerns about mildew, I installed louvres to ventilate all the lockers, and this never was a problem. I installed cabin fans, one in each sleeping cabin and two in the saloon.

It was necessary to stow spare diesel, gasoline (for the dinghy outboard), and propane tanks on the side deck in the cockpit area, lashed to the lower lifeline and toe rail. Margaret made weather cloths to screen this unsightly mess.

Carbon monoxide is a hazard that must be taken seriously aboard boats. I installed a carbon monoxide alarm wired into the boat's 12-volt electrical system. It was on a circuit that I had previously installed for some lighting without paying sufficient attention to wire gauge and distance. Consequently, there was enough voltage drop in the circuit to cause the alarm to emit a very loud beep whenever one of the lights on that circuit was turned on. (The device was designed to beep you when the voltage was too low for it to operate properly.) This got to be a problem, because we were jumping all over the place whenever one of those lights was turned on. I had to disconnect it.

I also installed a smoke detector (battery operated), but it went off whenever Margaret made toast in the morning. We couldn't deal with this either, so I disabled it too. Oh well.

Mail and Mail Drops

We used the US Postal Service, marinas, and friends and family for mail drops. We had mixed results with the Post Offices and 100% success with the marinas and friends and family. The Post Offices that failed miserably to perform the simple task of receiving properly addressed mail and delivering it over the counter were Delray Beach, Florida 33444 and Beaufort, South Carolina 29902. In Delray Beach we spent a half day and over $25 in cab fare chasing around town at the direction of incompetent USPS employees (the package was right there all the time). At Beaufort, the package was sitting in plain view in the back of the post office during the entire three days that USPS employees insisted that it had not arrived.

Nevertheless, most Post Offices will do a good job at this. The *Waterway Guide* books (Northern, Mid-Atlantic, and Southern) list the Post Offices along the ICW that are within walking distance of the waterfront. Packages should be addressed like this:

Your Name
Aboard (name of vessel)
c/o General Delivery
Post Office and Zip Code   HOLD FOR ARRIVAL

With marinas, it would be the same, except c/o the marina and its address.

Charts and Guides

The *Waterway Guide Chartbooks (New York Waters, Chesapeake and Delaware Bays, Norfolk to Jacksonville, Jacksonville to Miami,* and *Lower Florida and the Keys)* were our primary navigational references. In addition, we carried a collection of full-sized charts covering such areas as New York Harbor, the New Jersey shore, Norfolk Harbor, and the North Carolina Sounds. *The Waterway Guide Chartbooks* are no longer published, but there is another, similar, series. In the Chesapeake we used *Charts of the Chesapeake,* a chartbook published by *Chesapeake Bay Magazine,* and its companion book, *Guide to Cruising Chesapeake Bay.*

In the realm of books, we used the three *Waterway Guides (*The "Walters": *Northern, Mid Atlantic,* and *Southern)* which are published annually. On the Intracoastal Waterway itself, the small, spiral-bound book by Jan and Bill Moeller titled *The Intracoastal Waterway Norfolk to Miami: A Cockpit Cruising Handbook* was truly indispensable. We used the *Waterway Facilities Guide,* an annual publication that lists many marinas up and down the coast, and the *Light List and Waypoint Guide* published by International Marine.

We also carried *A Cruising Guide to the Northeast's Inland Waterways* by the Rumseys, *Cruising the Chesapeake by Shellenberger,* Claiborne S. Young's cruising guides to coastal North Carolina, South Carolina, Georgia, and Eastern Florida, and Frank Papy's *Cruising Guide to the Florida Keys.*

For a number of years preceding the cruise I had cut articles on the Intracoastal Waterway and destinations along the way out of *Cruising World* and *Coastal Cruising* magazines. In plastic sleeves and organized geographically into four loose-leaf binders, these were also in *Witch of Endor's* library.

We had one helluva lot of information on board. I did not keep close track, but I guess the charts and guides for our adventure represented an investment of around $800.

Boat Insurance

We were traveling between an area of low cost insurance (Great Lakes) and the highest cost area in the country (South Florida). There are three or four cost zones between Lake Erie and South Florida, and they get progressively more expensive as you move south. Our normal annual rate in the Great Lakes is about $400; our annual rate in South Florida would be approximately $1,000.

By prior arrangement with Boat/US, our insurance carrier, we called them as we left one zone and entered the next—as we went under the George Washington Bridge, as we were leaving the Chesapeake, and so on down to leaving Jacksonville (We reversed this on the way home). This kept us covered at minimum cost, compared to paying the South Florida rate for the entire year.

First Aid Kit

Toolin' around on a sailboat carries high risk of injury, and for much of the year we would be 12 to 24 hours away from medical care. Here are the contents of our on-board first aid kit:

ACE bandages (2)
Betadine—for cleansing wounds and scrapes
Sterile gauze pads—several sizes
Gauze bandage, 2" roll
Tweezers and sharp scissors
Alcohol swabs
Adhesive tape
Hydrogen Peroxide
Bandaids
Tylenol
Dramamine
Eye patch—to prevent further damage to an
            injured eye while getting to an
            emergency room
Burn Ointment
Eye Ointment
Anbesol—for toothache pain
Antihistamine
Hydrocortisone cream
Diarrhea medicine
Thermometer
Maalox
Coricidin
Emetrol

All this stuff was stored in plastic storage boxes, which seal out air and moisture. It still is. We didn't have a single medical emergency, not even a minor one. But here, home in Bay Village 18 minutes from the Cleveland Clinic, we're ready for *anything.*

Spares

We carried a spare pump for the boat's pressure water system (not used), a head rebuild kit (used and replaced—ugh!), and a supply of the usual diesel engine parts—water pump impellers and gaskets, belts, and fuel, oil, and air filters.

Mechanical Ability

You don't need a lot of mechanical knowledge and aptitude to undertake this kind of voyage on a sailboat, although obviously, the more you have the better you will be equipped for mechanical emergencies. My abilities in this area are marginal at best. Basic maintenance on a diesel engine (Changing oil, filter, water pump impeller, belts and hoses, and bleeding air from the fuel line) is pretty simple; but I never did bleed air, and I still don't feel competent to do so.

Important Gear

In addition to the items which you would normally expect to find on a sailboat, such as a compass and a VHF radio, a Waterway trip requires a hand-held VHF radio (or one installed at the helm), decent binoculars, and polarized sunglasses. Our binoculars have a built-in compass, a very useful feature enabling the person spotting distant aids for the helmsperson to indicate an approximate bearing so they can be found more quickly by sighting over the binnacle compass.

Polarized sunglasses are important. There are times when glare on the water prevents you from seeing what you need to see, and ordinary sunglasses are of little help.

Backpacks are mentioned in the narrative. Many shopping trips are on foot or bike, and one needs the additional capacity. It is amazing how comfortably a heavy load can be transported in this fashion. Bikes are also to be considered. We didn't bring bikes because we didn't have the room to store them, even the folding type, let alone the scratch—decent folding bikes are over $400 each.

In coastal cruising, it is essential to have knowledge of what the tides are doing in order to make judgments based on present and future water depths and current direction and speed. We carried a device called "Tidetracker", a hand-held computer that enabled one to quickly determine for the present moment and for some moment in the future what the tide and tidal current situation was or was going to be. It became indispensable to us—the alternative being working with the tide tables available in several publications, a tedious job at best.

The bad news is that "Tidetracker" is no longer made. The good news is that the reason it is no longer made is that this capability is now available as a feature of certain (and soon, I am sure, many) GPS units.

GPS is an extremely useful device to have on board for an extended coastal cruise. It tells you, among other things, where you are, and what course to steer to get where you want to go. One doesn't need GPS in canals and rivers, but in open sounds and bays, and of course in the ocean, is a marvelous thing to have. While a person undertaking a coastal cruise must have good boating skills and understand the basics of coastal piloting (knowledge of navigation aids, and working with charts, time, speed, and distance to plot position and course to follow), GPS makes all of this much simpler. The best arrangement (I believe) is to have a charting GPS installed below at the navigation station and a hand-held or helm-mounted GPS in the cockpit. With the price of these units dropping so drastically, this is quite feasible. And of course, having two on board reduces to an acceptable level the odds of being without one due to unit failure.

Our PFDs (Personal Flotation Devices) are of the suspender (SOS®) self-inflating type that doubles as a safety harness. I rigged jacklines along the toe rail cockpit to bow, and we had tethers enabling us to clip onto the jacklines when we left the cockpit to go forward. We used this gear when we were offshore or in open water during periods of rough weather.

Food and Such

(Once again, Margaret gets the last word!)

I would like to add just a few notes about food. First of all, it is important to remember that this was not an off shore ocean voyage, so we could get to a supermarket pretty much whenever we needed to. Most of the things we prepared were similar to what we have at home, with a few minor modifications. It just took a little bit of planning, because we didn't have as much storage space for back-up supplies as we do at home. We had more things like pastas, rice, and dried tortolini. We used dried sauce mixes; Lipton has dried pasta and rice with sauce products, which are pretty good, and of course, they store easily.

Bisquick is a necessity for pancakes, biscuits, and one dish "impossible" meals. It can serve as flour in a pinch. Small packets of mixes such as Betty Crocker, Jiffy, and Martha White are convenient. We used more canned and dried food than we do at home, because of storage and availability. Plum tomatoes keep the best without refrigeration. (Local produce is no bargain in Florida.)

Zip-lock bags are important aboard a boat, especially in the humidity of Southern coastal waters. Boxes of Bisquick, breakfast cereals, snack crackers and such are kept in zip-locks.

We always kept a couple of boxes of Parmalat milk in the food locker. This is a non-refrigerated liquid milk product (you cannot tell the difference between this and refrigerated milk), for use when we ran out of milk and couldn't get to a store. Many supermarkets carry this.

An electric fry pan with a high cover is a big convenience when you are plugged into shore power. Our stove has two burners and an oven, but there are times when the fry pan can serve as another burner. With a rack that fits, you can bake in it. I used the top of the navigation desk for the fry pan (on our boat this is adjacent to the stove), putting down folded newspaper and a towel to protect the desk surface from the heat, which gets extreme when you set it on high for an extended period.

A pressure cooker is a fuel-saving piece of equipment, as well as a good pan to use for frying chicken. Other useful items: plastic egg carton (from a boating supply store), folding dish-drying rack and a folding, stovetop toaster (from a camping supply store). It's a good idea to check out kitchen and camping stores for things like these.

We used washable dishes and tableware because disposables are costly, take up space, and make more trash; the same goes for place mats and napkins.

The best time to bake in the oven is on cold, rainy, miserable days—smells great and warms the cabin as well as the heart. Cockpit lunches underway were most often cheese and crackers and/or the little packaged cheese sandwich crackers or the peanut butter type (the best tasting are made by Frito-Lay). Sometimes Steve (he fixed lunch because I have difficulty working below while underway) would make sandwiches. Add fruit, cookies, and in cool weather a mug of steaming soup and you have a well-balanced meal.

For coffee, I used a small, four-cup French press. This was just right for Steve's morning coffee (I am a tea drinker). At home, Steve grinds his coffee and keeps it in the freezer. Our daughter Pam gave Steve a small manual coffee grinder for the trip, and although Steve asked me several times *not* to grind coffee for him, but to use ordinary supermarket ground coffee, he had nothing but fresh ground coffee for the entire year of our adventure. I guess this is my contrary nature. I would sit in the cockpit in the evening grinding coffee. Boy, he sure knows how to get his way!

Hmmm . . . .